Nina Bawden was born in London in 1925 and educated at Ilford County High School for Girls and Somerville College, Oxford. Her acclaimed career spans twenty adult novels, ten of which are published by Virago, and seventeen for children. For ten years she served as a magistrate, both in her local court and in the Crown Court. She has also sat on the councils of various literary bodies, including the Royal Society of Literature – of which she is a Fellow – PEN, the Society of Authors, and the ALCS, and is the President of the Society of Women Writers and Journalists. In addition she has lectured at conferences and universities, on Arts Council tours and in schools. Nina Bawden is married to Austen Kark, formerly Managing Director of the External Services of the BBC. They live in London and Greece. Nina Bawden was awarded a CBE in 1995.

THE WORKS OF NINA BAWDEN

NOVELS

Who Calls the Tune (1953)

The Odd Flamingo (1954)

Change Here for Babylon (1955)

The Solitary Child (1956)

Devil by the Sea (1958)

Just Like a Lady (1960)

In Honour Bound (1961)

Tortoise by Candlelight (1963)

Under the Skin (1964)

A Little Love, A Little Learning
(1965)

A Woman of My Age (1967)

The Grain of Truth (1969)

The Birds on the Trees (1970)

Anna Apparent (1972)

George Beneath a Paper Moon
(1974)

Afternoon of a Good Woman
(1976)

Familiar Passions (1979)

Walking Naked (1981)

The Ice House (1983)

Circles of Deceit (1987)

Family Money (1991)

CHILDREN'S BOOKS

The Secret Passage (1963)

On the Run (1964)

The White Horse Gang (1966)

The Witch's Daughter (1966)

A Handful of Thieves (1967)

The Runaway Summer (1969)

Squib (1971)

Carrie's War (1973)

The Peppermint Pig (1975)

Rebel on a Rock (1978)

The Robbers (1979)

Kept in the Dark (1982)

The Finding (1985)

Keeping Henry (1988)

The Outside Child (1989)

Humbug (1992)

The Real Plato Jones (1994)

PICTURE BOOKS

Princess Alice (1986)

In My Own Time

ALMOST AN AUTOBIOGRAPHY

Nina Bawden

A *Virago* Book

Published by Virago Press 1995

Reprinted 1997

First published by Virago Press Ltd 1994

Copyright © Nina Bawden 1994

A CIP catalogue record for this book
is available from the British Library

ISBN 1 86049 031 X

Printed and bound in Great Britain by
Clays Ltd, St Ives plc

Virago
A Division of
Little, Brown and Company (UK)
Brettenham House
Lancaster Place
London WC2E 7EN

To all my family and friends –
especially, perhaps, for Jean

William James Cushing = Edith Emily Croxen
(coach painter)　　　　(dressmaker)
　　　　　　　　　　　1860-1950

Achille Bennati　=　Jane Mabey
(ship's cook)　　　(widow; lodging-house
　　　　　　　　　　　keeper)

Ellalaine Ursula May ② = Mario Angelo = ① Helen Ward
(Judy)　　　　　　　　(aka Charles Mabey)
1898-1986　　　　　　　1886-1976

William Ewart
(Uncle Bill)

Margaret
(Aunt Peg)

Bridget

Peter　　Robin

Patricia
(sister Pat)

Austen Steven Kark ② = Nina = ① Henry Walton Bawden
(1926-　)　　　　　　(1925-　)

Perdita
(1957-　)

Niki
(1948-1982)

Robert
(1951-　)

CHAPTER ONE

Chinese Whispers

My mother was once long-jump champion of Norfolk. I have no evidence of this but I have always believed it to be true, and it would not have been, for her, an unlikely achievement: she was long-legged and athletic, still fit enough in her seventies to turn a neat cartwheel. Perhaps the fact, the truth, is recorded somewhere. If not, there is no one left alive to ask. I have to rely on what I remember.

All our stories begin before we are born. Not just the blue eyes or flat feet we inherit, but the stories we hear from uncles and aunts, from grandmothers and grandfathers. Even if oral history is no more reliable than the party game of Chinese whispers, everyone bringing to it their own subjective lumber of myths, half-truths, fancies and deceits, it is still these family stories that tell us who we are and help to shape our lives.

My maternal grandmother's name was Edith Emily. Born in Norfolk in 1860, she married William James Cushing, a carpenter and coach painter, and had four children: Billy, Peggy, Bridget, and Ellaline Ursula May, who was to be my mother. My grandfather, a keen theatre-goer, had named his youngest daughter after his favourite comedienne, Ellaline Terriss, or, at least, he had registered her birth in a variant of that name, but my grandmother preferred the name Judy, so Judy my mother became, and remained.

My grandmother was a dressmaker by trade. I can remember

sitting on her lap and feeling the tips of her fingers which were rough with pin pricks. But what drew me to her, as a child, was a feeling of kinship. I guessed that, like me, she was more interested in other people's lives than in her own. And as a result, although she had lived all her life in small market towns in East Anglia, she had never been bored. She had a brother-in-law, Harry, who had travelled the world and was the dullest man you could meet. It was as if he had never been anywhere, my grandmother said. Whereas she, Edith Emily, was surrounded by drama. Her friends, her neighbours, the women who came to be fitted for a dress in the front room of her cottage – in the private theatre of her imagination they all became creatures of infinite richness and complexity, characters in a never-ending story I seemed to spend most of my early years listening to.

My grandfather died when I was eight. My mother refused to take me to his funeral, which was a grief to me, chiefly because I fancied playing a touching part in the ceremony, laying a posy on his grave, and seeing people shake their heads and whisper sadly to each other as they observed tears shining in my eyes. My mother said, reproach-fully, 'You wouldn't want to see poor Granny crying, would you?' I suppose I denied it, but it was precisely what I did want to see; I was hungry for some real-life drama that could be seen and heard and stored away for future use.

My grandmother came to live with us for a while and later, when she moved into a small house in Romford, a bus ride away, I some-times stayed with her, to keep her company. I shared her billowing feather bed. We ate at odd times. We went to the cinema, often watch-ing the programme round twice; the main film, the 'B' feature, the news, and the main film again. We were usually there when 'God Save The King' was played at the end of the evening, and my grandmother always insisted we stay in our seats while the rest of the audience rose obediently. 'We don't stand for that family,' was all she would say in explanation, although one of my aunts later suggested that it might have something to do with an incident on a road near Sandringham when a minor royal had driven past my grandfather and splashed mud on his only suit. Other evenings we sat by the fire, sipping home-made blackcurrant wine which my grandmother affected to believe was non-alcoholic, while she told me stories about her girlhood and womanhood and the people she had known.

Her father had been a postman, her mother the local busybody – the wise woman, the midwife. When my grandmother was young, her mother had nursed the village through an outbreak of plague. (There were still outbreaks of plague in East Anglia in the 1870s.) My grandmother could remember her mother coming home, taking off her clothes in the outhouse and bathing in the heated copper before she came indoors. The doctor, who was frightened of infection, had leaned on her heavily, refusing, on one occasion, to attend a woman in labour because there was plague in the house next door. The birth was a difficult one, but by the time the doctor came, at last and reluctantly, my great-grandmother had delivered the baby and handed it, screaming, to its mother. When the doctor arrived and called from the bottom of the stairs, she stood at the top, with the afterbirth in a bucket. She said, 'I suppose you've come for your half-crown! Well, you can have this instead.' And she emptied the bucket over his head.

Edith Emily was proud to tell this story about her mother. She was anarchic and undeferential herself; entirely 'respectable' in her manners and behaviour, but not in her opinions. She was a small woman, with a tiny waist and delicate hands, but she was physically strong and apparently fearless.

One Harvest Fair, when she was an apprentice dressmaker, a suitor came after her with a shotgun. Of all the young men who hung around the draper's entrance to escort her home after work, or lingered in the church porch at the end of the service on Sunday, Saul was the one she had taken least account of. He was the gamekeeper's son, nineteen years old with a pasty face and long, narrow jaw, and he hardly ever spoke. He had left bunches of flowers on the low wall in front of her family's cottage, and once a basket of plover's eggs. Edith Emily took the eggs indoors to her mother but she left the flowers to wither.

'Fetch them indoors at least,' her mother said. 'He may be too quiet for you, but that's no reason to shame him.'

Edith Emily said, reasonably, 'If I don't want him, it's best that he knows it. And it's not just that he's quiet. There's something about him gives me the shivers.'

She was at the coconut shy with two little brothers when Saul appeared with the gun. She had her back to him. She had just won a coconut. The first thing she knew was the silence. Or the partial silence. One minute, the Fair was all busy bustle and laughter; the next, the only continuing sound was the tinny music of the merry-go-round floating thinly on the blue, evening air. Even that slowed and stopped as she turned, her coconut prize in her hands, and looked down the barrel of the gun.

No one was near. A shocked circle of townsfolk stood still and watching. In the yellow light from the naphtha flares, Saul's face was sickly pale. The gun trembled as his hands shook but it was steady enough for his dangerous purpose. He spoke into the awful, stunned silence. He said that if she wouldn't marry him, he'd kill her, then her brothers, and himself after. Behind him, the blacksmith took a step forward. And stopped. Saul said, 'And anyone who moves, I'll make a hole in him, too. I'll just ask the once more. Will you marry me, Edith Emily?'

'Say you'll marry him, Emily,' her mother hissed from the sidelines. No one else made a sound.

Emily looked at Saul carefully. Then she said, loud and clear, 'I wouldn't have you at any price, not if you were worth a thousand pounds a year. So you'd better put that gun back before your father misses it, or you'll be in trouble. Better still, give it to me.'

She was still holding her coconut. She gave it to her little brother beside her and held out her hand for the gun. And Saul gave it to her.

What happened to Saul, no one seemed to know. Perhaps he was marched off by the blacksmith and taken home to his father the gamekeeper, who kept a more watchful eye on his guns in the future. The story, as told by my mother (it is not one, as it happens, that my grandmother told me) said nothing about what happened after except in one romantic particular. A witness of this event, of Edith Emily's successful mixture of fearlessness, bravado and judgement of character, was a young coach painter, working in London, who had come to visit his family for the Harvest Fair, saw my grandmother as a high-spirited heroine (as, indeed, she saw herself all her life), and determined to marry her.

The fact that my mother did not know (or care to remember) what happened to Saul is significant. In her family archives the whole point of that story is that it ended in an idyllic marriage; a happy history passed down through the generations, told and re-told and sentimentalised in the process until my grandmother's marriage to her coach painter and my mother's childhood appear a little like a Victorian Christmas card. Snow falling gently on pretty children, cosily attired with muffs and fur tippets; welcoming light glowing softly in the cottage window. We know that indoors the fire will be lit, the table laid, the kettle on the hob, Mother waiting with a batch of mince pies hot from the oven. Father may have been dismissed from his job and gone to America but he sends minutely detailed postcards to his loving family and all will be well in the end.

Not that there is anything wrong in editing memories. There is always an alternative view and there is no undue virtue in 'honesty', which is often no more than another kind of selection. Why remember (for example) the coach painter's father, the tramp; such a shameful skeleton in a respectable family's cupboard that my mother always denied his existence. It is just possible that since she was the youngest child of the family, no one mentioned him to her. After all, my grandmother never mentioned him to me. I only found out about him in the 1970s, when I was in the middle of writing *The Peppermint Pig*, a children's book based on her story about the pig who had lived with her family when she was a child, a pet pig called Johnnie.

Johnnie was the runt of the litter. 'Peppermint' is a Norfolk version of 'peppercorn', as in peppercorn rent. My grandmother's mother had bought him from the milkman for a shilling when he was so small he could fit into a pint pot. He slept in the copper hole to begin with, then in front of the fire along with the jackdaw, the hen and the hedgehog. He grew, and had many adventures, and a good life until he went to the butcher's at the end of the year, an ending I had always thought beautifully sad. I had understood my grandmother when she said, 'Pigs were a poor person's investment in those days.

Who could afford to keep a great pig, eating its head off?' But she added that none of the children would eat bacon or sausage thereafter and Johnnie's hams hung from the beam in the kitchen until they got maggoty and were thrown away.

Johnnie had lived and died in the 1870s. For convenience, I chose to set his story thirty years later, in the time of my mother's childhood at the turn of the century. The essentials of country life had not changed. The rent of my grandmother's cottage was still a shilling a week; the same rent that her mother had paid. Cottagers still kept pigs; there were still travellers with dancing bears, solitary roadmenders chipping flints by the side of the road, Harvest Fairs where you could have a tooth pulled for sixpence – or watch someone else's tooth being pulled for a penny. Why bother researching historical details in libraries when I had access to living relations? My mother's memory was phenomenal, and her older siblings, my aunts and my uncle, although in their eighties now, were not far behind.

And there was another family story that had been told and re-told that would be interesting, I thought, to set down.

My mother was born in 1898. When she was about four years old, her father was unjustly accused of stealing from his employer, left his job, and went to America to work on the railway. William James was a gentle, bookish man, a theatre-lover, and perhaps more downwardly mobile than striving by nature; instead of taking a job as a carpenter or a painter on the railway, he found work with a cousin who was running a saloon in one of the gold-rush towns of California. (This cousin had changed his name for some reason and while he was employed by him William James changed his name, too. Why, no one knew, or, if they had known, they had forgotten.) Eventually, whatever his name was at the time, my grandfather became a valet to a travelling Englishman who brought him back to England.

During his absence, his family had gone to live in Swaffham, in Norfolk, a busy market town with a famous market square and a beautiful church with a fine wooden ceiling carved with flying angels. In the nineteenth century there was a regular winter 'season' in Swaffham; local squires would take a house in the town and introduce their daughters to society at a ball in the handsome Assembly Rooms which were curtained with crimson velvet and lit by hundreds of candles in chandeliers that tinkled – so my oldest aunt remembered – as the floor bounced under the dancing feet.

My mother spent her childhood in Swaffham and most of what she told me I put into my book: the sweets she ate, the games she played, as well as her memories of what had happened in the family while her father was in America. I changed some names. I called my mother Poll, and gave her two brothers instead of two sisters. And I made use of some of my Aunt Peg's and my Uncle Bill's memories, too – which included certain things my mother had omitted to mention.

The house my grandmother had rented in Swaffham was the one she was to live in for the next thirty years, until my grandfather died. I spent holidays there when I was a child. It had a small back room that smelled duskily of the geraniums, packed tight on the window-sill, and a long back garden with a woodpile and a tumbledown pigsty at the far end. My grandfather's sisters, Laura and Nan, lived in the house next door. When I knew them, they were both old and some-what alarming: Laura because she had had a stroke which made her dribble when she tried to talk, and Nan because she was red-faced and fierce and always hustled me out of the room when Great-Aunt Laura was tired, or wanted to use the commode.

But when Edith Emily first moved to Swaffham in 1902, Laura and Nan were still in their prime. Laura was the headmistress of the local school where Nan also worked, as an uncertificated teacher. They were determined and diligent women and ambitious for their brother's children. My mother was too young to be dragooned into learning, and her sister Bridget was not sufficiently clever, but towards Peg and Billy the aunts were autocrats, driving them relent-lessly up the educational ladder, setting fiercely high standards of manners and dress and general behaviour.

Aunt Laura made Peg wear Eton collars to school, stiffly starched instruments of torture that dug into the soft flesh of her neck, and when she complained that none of the other girls had to suffer so, Laura told her she ought to be glad to be 'different'. Peg wanted to be an actress and when she won a scholarship to the Royal Academy of Dramatic Art Laura and Nan offered to pay for her maintenance and lodgings in London. Unfortunately, at the end of the first year, Peg was commended by the Academy as 'the best vulgar comedian of her year', and her aunts refused to support her any longer. They had sent her to the Academy to become a tragedy queen, a Siddons or a Terry, not a comic actress, and certainly not a vulgar one. Peg went on the music halls for a while with an act that involved a man and a child and had some success until the child died. That was the end of her theatrical career; for the rest of her life she taught drama and dancing in private schools in Herne Bay in Kent; painted flower pictures and dug in her garden.

If the aunts had more success with their nephew, who went to the Hammond Grammar School and won a scholarship to Cambridge, it might be because they had a closer control over him when the family moved to Swaffham than they had over the girls. The terraced cottages had only three bedrooms, one of them little more than a cupboard (made even smaller when I knew it by a tin bath hanging on the back of the door) and so Bill lodged with his aunts next door. And, suffering as he did from their expectations of him, he found his single meeting with his paternal grandfather memorably gratifying.

He came down one morning to find an old tramp sitting by the fire and bawling at Laura and Nan to bring him a 'nice piece of belly pork', and to be quick about it. Bill was amazed. His aunts raised the roof if he brought in a speck of dirt on his shoes – and now they were scurrying about like frightened mice, waiting meekly on this filthy old man whose great smelly feet stank and steamed like a midden. Later, when the old man had gone, and he asked them about him, they said, in some surprise, as if he should have known, 'Why, Billy, that was your grandfather.'

Apparently the old man had been a blacksmith who had taken to drink and then to the road, and turned up to harass his children occasionally. He had gone to my grandfather's workplace to see what he could get out of him and he had been left briefly alone in the office. That was the day the money had been stolen and William James had been afraid they would send the police after his father. So when he was accused he said nothing and by the time his employer's son confessed to taking the money, the idea of going to America had taken root in his mind.

Years later, telling me about this episode, the memory of his formidable aunts reduced to daughterly subservience by this swashbuckling free spirit made my old uncle chuckle. Then he said that he had admired his aunts the more afterwards. The periodic appearances of their disreputable father cannot have gone unremarked in the town. And yet it had not damaged their dignity, nor their resolve to see their family rise up in the world; work hard, pass examinations, wear Eton collars.

Naturally, I put the tramp in my book where he fitted perfectly – the story falling into place around him as if he had been the missing piece of a jigsaw puzzle. I was pleased with the book when it was finished and I hoped my mother would be pleased, too: it was, in a way, a present for her, a daughterly tribute. Instead, to my astonishment she flew into a rage. How dare I present her, at her age, with a dirty, filthy, old tramp for a grandfather? Why, Aunt Laura and Aunt Nan would turn in their grave! I pointed out that they had put up with him when he was alive. And that, anyway, this was no sly fiction of mine but something my uncle, her *brother*, had told me. That made things worse. My mother never really forgave me, we simply stopped talking about it. But she never spoke to my uncle again.

It wasn't because he had lied to me. She admitted that he had told me the truth. She simply thought he should have said nothing. She preferred the past sanitised, untouched by anything she thought of as shameful. And besides, once the old tramp had been brought into the open, become common knowledge, she could no longer maintain quite so vehemently that her family were socially superior to my father's. Better educated, perhaps – one of my father's most bitter complaints against my Uncle Bill was that Billy had once corrected his pronunciation of the word *profile* – but in the respectability stakes honours were more or less even between an old tramp and an absconding Italian seaman.

The name that my father went by, the name that I assumed was his for almost fifty years of my life, was Charles Mabey. Born in 1886, he had two older brothers, both called Mabey, but their father, a lighterman on the Thames, had died long before my father was born. After her husband's death, my father's mother, a Scotswoman whose maiden name had been Jane Naylor, ran a lodging house for seamen in the East India Dock Road in London. My father once told me that she took in 'nobody below the rank of first mate', presumably to reassure me (and himself) that this was a high-class establishment, but one of her lodgers was only a cook; an Italian ship's cook called Achille Bennati. He married Jane a month before my father was born and, several years later, ran off with a much younger woman, a stewardess on a passenger liner.

Jane reverted to her first husband's name. My father was christened Mario Angelo Bennati but when he left school to be apprenticed to an engineering workshop in the London Docks, he decided to take the same name as his mother and brothers. From that time until his death in his ninetieth year, he was known as Charles Mabey. I have no idea where 'Charles' came from. By the time I found out about the ship's cook my father was well on in his eighties and had begun to look like an elderly Italian himself, with his beaky nose and a black beret permanently protecting his bald head from draughts. It was a beguiling thought that one of us might suddenly clap him on the shoulder and startle him. *Come sta, Mario Angelo?* – but it seemed indelicate to question him about his vanishing father. He might have preferred to forget all about him. After all, my mother had once hissed at me, 'Never ask your father to show you his birth certificate.'

At the time, I had simply been puzzled: I was about nine years old and this was not a question I had thought of asking. Suspicion (and the employment of an amiable genealogist I met at a party) came later; about twenty-five years after another family skeleton had tumbled out of the cupboard.

Both my parents, it seemed, had things they preferred to keep hidden. It was as if they had signed a mutual protection agreement. My father, ashamed of his vagabond Italian father, and apparently terrified of being asked to produce his birth certificate, deferred to my mother in her wish to keep his oldest child a secret from his second family.

My father was twelve years older than my mother. He had been married before and his first wife had died soon after their daughter was born. When he married my mother, his daughter Pat lived with them – or, to be more accurate, since my father was away more often than he was at home – she lived with my mother and, after I was born, with my mother and me.

My mother once told me – proudly, because she considered it to be her success story, not mine – that I had been clean and dry before I was a year old. I was born in January 1925, so this, my first memory, must have been towards the end of that year.

I had fallen down the stairs and was sitting on the stiff, prickly hairs of the doormat in the hall. I was wearing nappies – that is, I was conscious of a damp bulk between my thighs. Perhaps I was crying. I don't know. What I do remember is that there was another child there; a child with dark hair who was bigger than me. My mother was there as well. And she was angry.

At some point, when I was older (perhaps around the same time that I was advised not to ask my father for his birth certificate), I spoke to my mother about this strange memory and she became mysteriously agitated. She said I had 'too much imagination'. I knew this was a crime and said nothing more.

The truth, as eventually revealed by my sister, was comprehensible if not simple. Pat and I had been together on the upstairs landing. She went to the bathroom and I fell down the stairs. My mother accused her of pushing me. Pat says this wasn't true, and I believe her, but it was clearly the climax of family tensions of an obscure but passionate kind and my father, who for once was at home, took her away to live with two women cousins, one of whom was Pat's godmother. They went in a taxi, is what she chiefly remembers (a taxi being an exciting novelty) and our father gave her a box of chocolates to comfort her.

For the next quarter of a century Pat knew about me and about my two younger brothers, saw our photographs in our father's cabin when she went on board to see him when his ship was docked in Tilbury, but we knew nothing about her. We only met, at the end of the Second World War, because she insisted. My father would have lived his life out if he could, avoiding this kind of emotional trouble. He was a brave man but he found women a mystery, and when they made trouble, as my mother had obviously done about my sister, he preferred to take the easy road. I was twenty-six when my mother told me that I had a half-sister.

When, many years later, I thought of writing about this curious episode, I wrote it from my sister's point of view, not from mine, but all the same my children's book *The Outside Child* is an attempt to make sense of something that had happened to me when I was nine months old.

Nothing is ever so simple, of course. There are more ingredients in the gamey stew of family life than can be easily counted: the best anyone can do is to sniff and taste – and ask the right questions at the right time. The pity is that by the time the questions are clear, those who know the answers are usually dead. My Uncle Bill, my Aunt Peg, my father and mother were all dead before I learned (from my Uncle Bill's wife, my Aunt Isobel, who had outlived them all) that the parents of my father's first wife lived next door to my mother's parents, my grandmother and grandfather, and that my sister Pat's mother had been Isobel's best friend.

I was lucky to have known my grandmother, and lucky that she had a good memory and a talent for stories. And a robust common sense, too. Now I am older, and have become more interested in money than I used to be, there is one detail about the episode at the Harvest Fair that intrigues me. Edith Emily said that she wouldn't have Saul 'at any price', but then she put a price on her refusal. She wouldn't have him even if he were worth a 'thousand pounds a year'. This was a huge sum for a dressmaking apprentice in the 1870s to contemplate. For that amount of money a family could have not only a substantial house but a carriage and horses, a coachman, and at least three indoor servants. And, presumably, since my grandmother was accustomed to working for the gentry, even though at that age she was only sewing the buttons on their everyday dresses, she had some idea of the kind of income needed to keep up the style that they lived in. When I think of this story what I see is not just a gutsy young heroine but, in her ability to contemplate riches and reject them contemptuously, a person with a proper sense of her own value.

She was, after all, a poor girl. Though not dirt poor, not poverty stricken. The Romford house she lived in after my grandfather died was smaller than the one in which she had brought up her family (only two bedrooms, not three) but filled with the same furniture, most of it inherited from her own parents, from childless uncles and aunts, and it was all good, well-made stuff; bow-fronted chests of drawers, solid wardrobes and chairs, a fine, round, walnut table; pretty Staffordshire figures on the mantelshelf, brightly coloured rag rugs on the floor. A handsome jar that her brother-in-law (the despised and boring Harry) had brought back from China, served as an umbrella stand by the front door. She made clothes for herself, for her family and for her neighbours, as meticulously as she had once made clothes for the rich families of Swaffham. Once, she showed me her 'savings' – three new pound notes hidden among the lavender bags in her underwear drawer. I think I had asked if we could afford to go to the cinema and she was telling me not to worry because she had this money 'behind her'.

I believe that my grandmother was the only adult in my childhood whom I saw as another *person* – whole and complete. Most grown-ups, nice or nasty, were simply bundles of characteristics that might or might not be dangerous or useful to someone my age. They were beings to be watched and circumvented; I lived in the foothills of their lives as all children have to do.

My grandmother was older than any other grown-up around me which set her apart from them, and she didn't behave as they did. Specifically, she never assumed any authority over me, or at any rate none that I was conscious of. I thought of her as another child like me, albeit rather old. She was ready to play draughts, go to the cinema, more or less whenever I wanted. And she was always ready to tell stories – anxious to, indeed, which is probably the key to the comfortable relationship between us. What I wanted from her, she wanted to give me, and there was never any feeling on my part that she was tailoring her stories to fit my younger understanding; censoring them in any way. Like most children I had a liking for the gruesome which she was ready to indulge because it appealed to her as well. There was the story about the farmer who shut his wife in the pigsty at night and drove the pigs up to the bedroom. And the one about 'poor Willie', the only surviving child of one of my great-grandmother's neighbours.

Poor Willie's mother had had other children but they had died soon after birth and been buried in the back garden. The doctor (the same doctor who had arrived too late at the lying-in to pick up his money) muttered a warning. He couldn't look the other way for ever. If the next one died, the law would have to be alerted. And that would mean prison for poor Willie's dim-witted mother.

My great-grandmother kept a sharp watch but she missed the next birth; the first she knew of it was when she passed by the cottage and saw a dead baby lying on the windowsill. She knocked on the door and was told by her simple (and innocent) neighbour, 'I did put it on the chest of drawers but Willie would play with it.'

My grandmother had a deep voice for such a small and feminine woman and if I close my eyes I can hear her tell the best story of all; my favourite, my brother's favourite, my children's favourite . . .

Do you remember my telling you about old Granny Greengrass, how she lost her finger? Well, it was chopped off at the butcher's when she was buying half a leg of lamb. She had pointed to the place where she wanted her joint to be cut, but then she decided she wanted a bigger piece and pointed again. Unfortunately, Grummett the butcher was already bringing his sharp chopper down. He chopped straight through her finger and it flew like a snapped twig into a pile of sawdust in the corner of the shop. It was hard to tell who was more surprised, Granny Greengrass or the butcher. But she didn't blame him. She said, 'I could never make up my mind and stick to it, Mr Grummett, that's always been my trouble . . .'

CHAPTER TWO

─────────◆─────────

Before the War

There was a wooden trellis grown over by pale pink cabbage roses outside the kitchen door. On the concrete, by the step, I sat in a soft-sided wicker basket and looked up to see the house slowly falling on top of me. At some time I must have understood this was an illusion brought about by wind and flying clouds because I can remember the exquisite torment of daring myself to look upwards at the moving sky while knowing all the time (though never quite believing) that I was safe from harm.

Beyond the rose trellis there was grass, daisies and dandelions, and clumps of pink, stalky flowers called lords and ladies growing in the flanking beds. At the end of the long lawn there was another trellis and beyond that, a summer house that smelt deliciously of creosote, and four new apple trees, their thin trunks painted white. I had a patch of earth there and made little cakes in pots, earth mixed with icing sugar, that were interesting to eat, though gritty on the tongue.

I had a new brother. High above me, a shadow spoke; my aunt, my tall Aunt Peg. 'Someone's nose is going to be out of joint.' Another day, I sat in an armchair, right back in the seat so that my feet, in white socks and blue sandals, stuck straight out in front of me, and watched my mother feeding him and asked her if it hurt. She said, 'You must be a good girl, and do what you're told, or he might drain Mummy to death.'

He was christened Peter James. My tall aunt held him in the

church and gave his names. Peter was 'good' – which meant he didn't cry when the vicar took him from my aunt and dribbled water on his head. I stood on the steps of the font and peered into the basin. 'Can you see a fish, little girl?' the vicar asked. I liked him because he didn't smile; it made the joke a private one, just him and me. I said, unsmiling, in the same grave voice, 'No, but I saw a whale.' And the other silly grown-ups laughed.

Older, Peter sat on the rug before the fire and I played with him, picking up wooden bricks in my mouth and growling like a dog to make him laugh. Peter had curly hair and wore smocks made for him by my dressmaker grandmother. People said, 'What a pretty baby! What a beautiful child! That hair is wasted on the boy!' If they noticed me they just said, 'Funny little monkey face.'

Later, I went to school; a private school in a double-fronted house with dusty laurels in the garden and smelly lavatories with no proper seats. There were no bolts on the doors and sometimes bigger children opened them and sniggered at you, sitting there. I wore a brown uniform, a silky gym slip in the summer, stiff serge in the winter, and hats with sharp elastic that made deep, itchy ridges underneath the chin. Except for the lavatories, I quite liked this school until I was singled out for special treatment.

I had always made up stories and told them to myself and to my brother. Although I could read, I couldn't write well enough to satisfy myself and so I drew my stories as a picture book; little, crayoned figures acting out my fantasies and observations. Unfortunately for me, when I was five years old, my tall Aunt Peg, who taught art as well as drama, submitted some of my drawings to the Royal Drawing Society and they were commended and exhibited. I remember being taken to this exhibition and being handed a piece of stiff paper by a beaming and obviously well-intentioned grown-up, and though I knew I must smile and say thank you, I was confused. My nose was level with the glass table tops where the winning entries were displayed but, as far as I remember, no one explained that my pictures were among them, nor lifted me to show me what was there. On the other hand I was aware that I had done something to please my mother and since that was the main object of my life, I was content enough.

My mother, eager to nurture the slightest spark of talent, decided I should be given extra lessons. An art teacher came twice a week at the end of afternoon school to teach the older girls and I was made to join them. To be thrust upon the sneering attention of huge teenagers with enormous busts and smelly armpits was a nightmare on its own. To make it worse, the purpose of this torment was incomprehensible to me. When I drew my pictures, I drew the people I saw in my own head. I failed to see the point of drawing an apple and a pear, or a daffodil in a milk bottle, which was apparently the sort of exercise expected, and although, being willing by nature, I always did my best, the results were pitiful. I didn't need the art teacher, who seemed to be forever peering over my shoulder, to tell me so. I could see it for myself. In the end I said, in explanation, or despair, 'I don't draw bottles. I only draw *stories.*'

'Well, Nina, we have to learn to walk before we can run, don't we? Even if we win prizes, that doesn't mean no one can teach us anything, does it?'

I have no memory of what this woman looked like but I can recall her voice exactly. Not because of her flat, Essex vowels, what my mother, correcting my own diction, called 'lazy and common', although I registered this mark against her, but the nauseating blend of patronage and triumph in her tone. It cannot have been the first time I had encountered this kind of adult-to-infant put-down, but it was the first time it had really stung.

It would be nice to report that I gave a withering response. Instead, I burst into tears, which was probably more effective punishment for a part-time teacher whose employment (in a small private school in a far from prosperous suburb) was almost certainly precarious. I didn't often cry and once started found it hard to stop. I ran home, sobs growling in my chest and turning into painful, jarring coughs. By the time I flung myself upon my mother, I was hot, hysterical, and plainly ill.

I had whooping cough. I had to stay at home for the remainder of the term. It seemed a miraculous deliverance. 'Of course, we lose the fees, that can't be helped,' I heard my mother say to someone on the landing, outside my room. 'But it's a shame about the art classes, she was getting on so well.'

I prayed to God that the art teacher would die before I was well again. Her death was the only way out that I could think of. Whether God took heed, I never knew, but as I had been told at Sunday School, He moved in mysterious ways. When I was getting better, out of bed and able to go into the garden as long as I was bundled up around the chest, my mother told me that I wasn't going back to my old school but to the state elementary school. 'A bit further away, and across the main road, but you're old enough now. And next year Peter can go with you.'

The elementary school was a couple of quiet residential streets away. The 'main road' was the bus route; apart from buses it carried little heavy traffic, and only the smallest children, the first-year Infants, were taken to school by their mothers. From six or seven we all walked unaccompanied; dawdling, jumping cracked paving stones, pulling faces at houses where we suspected people watched us from behind their curtains, and, when we reached the main road, playing Last Across.

The school was Victorian, built of yellow London brick and shiny dark blue stone, with high narrow windows, stone stairs, and outside lavatories. These were just as nasty as the ones at my other school but, being older and more continent, I didn't mind so much. Nothing in my experience, however, had prepared me for the savage anarchy of the playground. Until a teacher rang the bell at the beginning of morning or afternoon school or at the end of break, you had to watch your back. I had to watch mine with extra care. I was no better dressed than anyone else but I was thought to give myself airs because I took a clean handkerchief to school every day and, nagged by my mother, spoke more clearly than most people did. There was one particular girl, fat-faced and piggy-eyed, who fell upon me every morning as I appeared in the playground. Bigger than I was, taller and heavier, she hurled me to the ground, seized bunches of my hair and thudded my head up and down on the concrete. I fought back but I always got the worst of it and was always in trouble, for going into school with dirty hands and face, for going home without my hair ribbon or with a torn skirt or blouse. Pride prevented complaint, or even explanation, but one morning at break, when we had drunk our milk, I cracked the neck of my empty bottle on the step and threatened to jab it into her hateful, piggy face.

She left me alone after that. So did other bullies. My reputation (undeserved, because unless goaded beyond endurance I was actually quite timid) must have spread abroad. When bigger boys amused themselves by pulling my brother, Peter, round the playground by his ears, I only had to turn up and shout, to put a stop to it.

I felt no resentment against the pig-eyed girl; on the contrary, once I had triumphed, I found myself quite well disposed towards her, even charitable. We paid a halfpenny a day for our mid-morning milk, and some of the poorer children could not afford even this small sum, my fat and thuggish enemy among them. I told my Auntie Aggie (not a real aunt, my mother's friend and my godmother, who was living with us at the time) about this 'poor girl', not mentioning how roughly she had treated me and glorying in my own forbearance, and Auntie said that she would give me the milk money to take to school and I could pay for her.

It was, looking back, a sweeter and more lasting revenge than shoving a broken bottle in her face. Every Monday I handed over fivepence to the teacher, who called out both our names as she marked them in the milk book. My enemy said nothing, although she drank the milk. It didn't occur to me that I had humiliated her; I just thought her dreadfully ungrateful. 'She never says thank you,' I complained importantly, talking to my best friend of about a week, and another girl who sometimes joined us as we walked to school. This girl said, 'That sort of person never does. She's from the council estate. Those people don't have manners.'

I was embarrassed by this crude remark. But it was my best friend who replied to it. 'That's a snobbish thing to say,' Jean said. 'You can live on the council estate and have good manners. She doesn't say thank you because she has a stutter, that's the only reason.'

My best friend's father was a 'thousand-a-year-man'. In the thirties, in our suburb, this was riches – more precisely, in my best friend's case – a big house opposite the park, a telephone, a car – and for some time after I was fully grown I saw £20 a week as the kind of salary to aim at. Even later, in the fifties, it seemed a safety net below which it could be dangerous to fall.

Although my parents were not poor in any real sense – we always had clothes and warmth and food – my father had a fear of poverty that to some extent infected all of us. (It infected me, at any rate.) He was a marine engineer with the P & O Company, a chief engineer by the 1930s, but no one's job was secure in those days and Merchant Navy engineers were on the beach in their hundreds. It was dangerous to take even a few days' leave between voyages and my father was away at sea all my childhood. We only had one family holiday, at Camber Sands the summer I was ten; other years he was afraid to leave his ship. He had been born in the East India Dock Road, left school at eleven, worked as an apprentice in the daytime and went to evening classes at the People's Palace (now Queen Mary and Westfield College) in the Mile End Road, at night. When our mother bought (for twelve-and-six a week) the house where I was born, he was at sea, somewhere off the coast of Australia. By the time he came home, the deed was done, the contract signed – and he was terrified. My mother said he wept. He earned three pounds a week; twelve-and-six was almost a quarter of his income. It was not so much the money as the responsibility! Suppose the chimney blew off? Who would pay to repair it?

Our house was one of thousands like it built between the wars: semi-detached, with a narrow side passage where the dustbins were kept, two living rooms, one where we ate and played and a best front room, three bedrooms, a thin kitchen, a bathroom-and-lavatory, and a long garden. My best friend's house had two more bedrooms, a small but separate lavatory, and a garage. Both houses were sound enough, our chimney never did blow off, but they had no architectural distinction; they were breeding boxes in a dullish suburb on the eastern edge of London where the town petered out in a waste of dreary housing estates and ruined countryside. We lived near the London Docks, but not near enough to enjoy the excitement and bustle of great ships coming and going. All the houses were alike: lace curtains at the windows and, sometimes, heavier drapes hung with the right side facing outward, to impress the street.

My mother, who had had such a happy childhood in the country, made it clear to me that our suburb was featureless and ugly and that no one but a fool or a dullard would live there if they had any choice in the matter. I cannot think that this opinion endeared her to our neighbours but perhaps she never told them what she thought of them. And, indeed, I only understood her when I was older. Before the war, my personal cartography of Goodmayes, Ilford, Essex, was a treasure island map of drama and discovery.

Take these twelve-and-sixpenny houses. There must have been about sixty of them in our street, all identical except for a bungalow at one end where the purple-tongued chow dog lived with his owner, a man whose head hung sideways on his neck and trembled as he walked. When I was eight or so, each of these houses was a theatre, all the more exciting because of the shrouding curtains and the air of prim respectability with which their inhabitants emerged to face the street. By that time, I had read through my grandmother's shelf of Sunday School Prizes; Victorian children's novels, strong on moral uplift and drama, like *Jackanapes*, and *Christie's Old Organ*, and *On Angel's Wings*. I found these books more satisfying than the flimsy tales of fairies and talking animals that were the literary fodder on offer in the children's department of the local public library. (Fortunately, when I was ten, I made friends with the librarian and was allowed to use my junior ticket in the adult library.) The people in my grandmother's books suffered long and hard; they were hunchbacks and consumptives, they starved, fell ill and took a long time dying. To begin with, when I wrote stories or plays, either to be performed at school or for the toy theatre Auntie Aggie had bought me, my characters were as different from the bank clerk, the fishmonger, or the cinema manager in our street, as I could make them. They were pirates, elephant hunters in Africa, princesses in disguise. But when I grew bored with what I began to see as a kind of falsity – as forced and unreal in its way as tales of talking animals – I turned a thoughtful gaze on to our neighbours. In books, *nobody* lived uneventful lives. They lost their money, killed each other, went to prison. It seemed to me unlikely that our neighbours were immune to such interesting disasters.

The dramas I devised for them were always tragic or romantic; I was too young for comedy. Mr and Mrs Smith, the elderly couple who lived next door had a radio they played so loudly that we could sometimes hear the news through the adjoining wall. For years, this was a great advantage for us when we wanted to listen to something important like the Boat Race. (We had no wireless of our own until the abdication of Edward VIII when my mother bought one so that we should hear the uncrowned king renounce his throne. 'Hark the herald angels sing, Mrs Simpson's pinched our king,' was what we sang in the playground, but our mother took it all more solemnly. She said it was a turning point in English history and we should listen carefully so that we could tell our children about it later on.)

I knew Mr Smith was deaf but I decided that deafness was just a convenient excuse. I had been reading *Jane Eyre*, given to me as an eighth birthday present by my Auntie Peg. Obviously, if you had a madwoman living with you, her ravings could be conveniently drowned by the wireless turned up loud. No one I knew had ever been invited inside the house next door. What did they have to hide?

I had never been invited either, but I was in the habit of slipping through a gap in the fence and pestering Mrs Smith for water biscuits which she crisped up in the oven for me. I would sometimes say that I was hungry; that I'd had no breakfast; that my mother was too poor to buy food to feed us. (Remembering this years later, I was shocked when my six-year-old son did the same thing, not because he told our neighbour he was hungry, but because she didn't tell me what was happening for a long time and when she did, watched me with a sly and doubtful air. Until that moment I had imagined that Mrs Smith was like the vicar, joining with me in a game; now, suddenly and too late, I wasn't sure!)

All that I had ever seen of the Smiths' house was the kitchen where I waited for my water biscuits and, just once, the narrow entrance hall beyond, where there was a picture called *When Did You Last See Your Father?* hanging on the wall. (I had told Mrs Smith we had been doing Roundheads and Cavaliers at school and she had showed me this picture, of a Cavalier boy in a lace-collared suit being interrogated by a group of fierce Cromwellians.)

I thought I might need to go to the lavatory. That would get me upstairs and if I was quick about it I could peek into the bedrooms. But when I asked, Mrs Smith said, 'Then you'd better run back, dear. I'll keep your biscuit for another time.' I said, 'But I need to go *badly*,' and this time she turned on me sharply with a disapproving, pursed expression. 'It's not nice to use other people's bathrooms. I don't know what you're thinking of.'

I was convinced. There was only one reason why someone who was not absolutely demented would respond like this to such a simple and politely put request. If not an actual madwoman, there must be some sort of prisoner kept secretly upstairs; a deformed or loony child, perhaps, like Poor Willie in my grandmother's story about dead babies. I was sure I had heard mysterious thumps some nights; queer moanings in the chimney . . .

I thought up similarly derivative predicaments for other people in our street. The only thing that interests me about these unoriginal stories now is the curious way some of them became rooted in my imagination so that years later I believed them to be true. During the London Blitz my mother shared an Anderson shelter with the Smiths. At some time after the war she was talking about them, telling me something that had amused her (I think it was that Mr Smith was such a proper gentleman, he refused to remove his tie while she was in the shelter) and I said, without thinking, 'So you got to see who it was, at last?' Then, realising what I had said, I shook my head and laughed. 'Wasn't there some story about some old relation tucked away. Or am I muddling them up with someone else?'

It was not altogether surprising that I should have invented where I didn't know. People in that kind of lower-income suburb were almost obsessionally private in a way not easily intelligible today. Children visited each other, were asked to tea, but a good many childless adults, although they might chatter in a friendly way over the garden fence, were careful whom they asked into their homes. It was perhaps something to do with necessary penny-pinching, or privacy hard won: for most, including my own mother, the buying of a house was a fairly bold adventure.

*

I was fascinated by other people's houses. Not because I was particularly sociable but because I was passionate to know how other people lived. In our household there was my mother and her visitors; her friends from teaching, Auntie Aggie, and from time to time her sisters, Peg and Bridget, and my grandmother. Except for my brother, nothing but women – or *harpies* as my father called them in his old age, complaining to my husband about the way they had ruled his family's life.

Someone once pointed out to me that my children's books were full of absent fathers though as far as I remember I didn't consciously miss mine. His absence was accepted and explicable; not the social embarrassment it might have been if my mother had been unmarried or divorced. But I do remember that when my father's cousin, Uncle Stanley, came to see us, what a difference it made to have a man around.

Everybody brightened up. Every woman in the house, however old or young. Or so I thought – now I wonder if it was only me. Certainly my mother sometimes muttered that Stanley should pay more attention to his own wife instead of dancing attendance on other people's, which I thought ungracious since he always brought her flowers or chocolates, and often presents for me and Peter, too. When I was twelve or thirteen, he gave me my first typewriter, a chattery, clattery and wonderfully reliable machine I used for years.

If the way he made me feel is anything to go on, Stanley was attractive to females of all ages and I would guess attracted by all ages too. He was sexy, but in a comfortable and liberating way that was not in the least threatening. He was dark-eyed, dark-haired and healthy looking, with a sweetly curved, full mouth; he usually turned up at tea time (what we called high tea, between five and six o'clock) and although I cannot recall a single thing he said, I remember that he always made us laugh. Sometimes he stayed as late as nine o'clock and after he had gone my mother would crossly chivvy me to bed and say she never knew a man for wasting time like Stanley.

Uncle Stanley was the first man for whom I felt a sexual flutter. Jean's father, Uncle Hedley, was the first person to show me that it was possible to have a rational discussion outside the pages of a book;

possible, indeed, to disagree with someone without flaring up with indignation as my mother usually did when I contradicted her.

'Uncle' and 'auntie' were the courtesy titles we gave to those grown-ups who would have thought Mr or Mrs too formal, and the use of their Christian names plain cheeky. Uncle Hedley was English deputy manager of the Belgian Bank in the City; he had started there as an office boy at the age of fourteen and risen as high as he could go, because the manager had to be Belgian. He was totally unlike Stanley; tall and quiet, with long front teeth and a nervous blink. He had been brought up in an orphanage and I thought that was probably why he was so shy; the free and easy bustle of his family life was still strange to him.

I didn't pay him much heed to begin with. Jean's mother, Auntie Beryl, a plump, merry, determined lady who sang in the Methodist church choir and insisted that her children each learned a different musical instrument, was obviously the pivot of the household and the person to pay attention to. Since I had decided that Jean was to be my best friend, it was more important that her mother should approve of me than that her father should.

I suspect Auntie Beryl looked me over. My father's job was not as *professional* as Uncle Hedley's, since an engineer worked with his hands, but my mother was a trained teacher, which counted for something in the scales, and she had taught me to speak well. And, anyway, Auntie Beryl was a good, warm-hearted woman; once a child had played in her house, sat at her table, she was part of the family, to be fed, protected and encouraged. (If it had not been for Jean's mother I would not have gone to Oxford: it was she who talked to my head-mistress, filled out the application for the county grant, arranged for me to take the entrance examination and then wrote to my mother to tell her what she'd done.)

Uncle Hedley brought home huge bags of foreign stamps once or twice a month, and emptied them out on to the dining table where Jean and I sometimes did our homework together. He may have pointed out a particularly interesting or colourful example that we might otherwise have missed, and showed us where it came from on the map, but mostly he left us to it unless we asked him something.

Until one evening when he came in and found us talking about mad people's brains.

There still is a famous psychiatric hospital at Goodmayes, specialising in schizophrenia. In my childhood, it was just 'the lunatic asylum', one of those big, handsome, old asylums that had been built outside big cities in the nineteenth century by rich philanthropists. There were high railings around the large and well-kept grounds, the kind of railings you would expect around a prison or a cage, and it was this that intrigued us. Lunatics were dangerous, as everyone knew, but there were quite wide gaps between the railings; a *thin* lunatic could easily get out!

Someone – not I, nor Jean – had the answer to this question. Lunatics had enormous brains and big heads as a result, so they couldn't get out through the railings or their heads would stick. The person who produced this information knew that it was true because her father worked in the laboratory in the hospital and had told her that the brains were there for anyone to see; the huge, grey, wrinkled brains of dead lunatics, pickled in big jars.

As we walked home, Jean said she didn't believe this girl. Passing the asylum as we did from time to time, we had seen the lunatics, walking in the grounds, and they looked just like ordinary people; their heads the same size as ours. I argued that those people might have been ordinary lunatics and that it was only the dangerous ones who had big heads, and they were kept inside the asylum in locked and padded cells.

Jean said nothing, which was often her habit when she disagreed, and usually I didn't mind, taking silence as a victory of a sort for me. But this time, perhaps because I was frightened, I didn't let it drop. And so, when Uncle Hedley came into the dining room that evening (either with more stamps, or to look something up in the encyclopaedia which was kept in a bookcase in this room) he heard me raving on about giant-headed mad people escaping from the hospital at night and how Jean ought to *care*. She might not mind about dying herself but she had a sister, and a baby brother.

Uncle Hedley didn't say, as most adults would have done, 'What's all this nonsense about?' but simply sat there, at the table, until one of us explained. And then, in a gentle and considering voice, he said he did not *think* it could be true; that the only unfortunate people with big heads that he had heard about were called hydrocephalics and they were harmless. Then he talked about the sizes of brains in general, and their relation to body weight, and to their function. I think Jean went away at some point – called away by Aunt Beryl to practise her piano, probably – but Uncle Hedley went steadily on. He told me more about brains than I needed or wanted to know, which was calming in itself, and said that if I was interested, answers to most questions could be found in the encyclopaedia, which I was welcome to use any time I liked.

I must have been ten or eleven then. We were in the top form of the elementary school and about to face the terrifying ordeal of the scholarship which my mother had convinced me was equivalent to Divine Judgment; you either passed and flew up to Heaven, or failed and tumbled down to Hell.

I read a great deal and could write quite fluently. Sometimes the teacher said my essays were good, and read them to the class. I had won a prize from the Lifeboat Association for a story about Grace Darling. Like the prize from the Royal Drawing Society, it was a disappointing piece of paper. I had even written a play that had been performed in the school assembly hall. Written during my African period, this was a tale of elephant hunters, a bad one and a good, searching for the elephant's graveyard; the good hunter for some noble purpose that escapes me now, the bad one to steal the ivory and make his fortune. Along the way the bad hunter fell into a tiger trap (I knew there were no tigers in Africa but thought lions were insufficiently frightening) thus presenting the good hunter with a moral problem, the purpose of the play. Should he rescue the bad hunter or not? I don't remember the resolution. All I remember is a line I had written for the bad hunter to cry out in despair. 'Help me, Carruthers, I have broken my confounded leg." When I wrote this line I had thought it sophisticated. Hearing it spoken publicly, I knew that it was irrecoverably bad. When, at the end, the headmistress said, 'And now we must give a special clap for Nina because she wrote this play all by herself,' I cried wildly, 'No, no I didn't, I told a lie, I found it in a book.'

It was the end of my career as a playwright. I knew from then on that I could never endure the public shame and grief. But according to my mother, if I failed the scholarship, I would have no career at all and no future worth speaking of. I would have to go to the secondary modern school and then into a factory.

I thought, privately, that to work in a factory would not be so bad. There were girls in my class who had fathers and brothers and mothers and sisters who worked at Ford's in Dagenham and they seemed to lead perfectly bearable, indeed often enviable, lives. Some of the fathers had cars. Even some of the mothers drove. They all went to the cinema and away on holiday more often than my family, and they stayed in hotels or boarding houses, not as we did, with Aunt Peg. When they went to the seaside at Southend they were allowed to play on the main beach near to the Fun Fair, while we had to go to what my mother called 'the better end' and paddle through thick, shiny, toe-sucking, crab-scuttling mud before we could reach the sea. And they all had beautiful shop cakes for their birthday teas instead of the shaming home-made cakes covered with hundreds and thousands that my mother made for me. But I knew better than to say that I would be happy to work in a factory. I knew what the answer would be. 'Oh, so you want to live the rest of your life on a council estate! I thought you had a little more in you than that, but if that's all you want . . .'

I said, forlornly, 'I can do English. I'm quite good at English. It's just *sums* I can't do.'

Or any kind of mathematical calculation except the simplest. I knew that for some people numbers had shape and meaning. I knew that Jean could *see* numbers as she could *see* music; numbers made patterns inside her head as poetry did inside mine. But they were a foreign language to me; I couldn't crack the code and after a while boredom took over and I no longer wanted to.

My mother decided she would coach me. I sat at the kitchen table after tea and snivelled over long division. I found it unimaginably difficult and she grew increasingly frantic. My brother, Peter, could add and subtract and divide, and was good with his hands, but *he* was backward at reading. It must have seemed to my unfortunate mother that she had given birth to two morons who would never be able to make their way in the world. She had just had a late third child, my younger brother, Robin, and was having to look after the three of us more or less alone. My grandmother came and sewed for us, and Auntie Aggie gave us treats, visits to London, tea at a Lyon's Corner House and *Peter Pan* or *Where the Rainbow Ends* at Christmas, but my mother had no one to share the anxiety she felt about our future. One evening, when I had been particularly stupid, she broke down in tears and said, 'Oh, Nina, what will become of you if you can't do a simple little sum like that?'

I think that some of the time I could have done the sums if I had not been paralysed with fear of failing – not failing the exam, but failing her. I know that when the dreaded day arrived, I was suddenly quite light-hearted with relief, and afterwards, comparing notes with Jean, thought it might be possible that I had got a few questions right. But at home, during the next weeks, I was too conscious of my mother's silent, waiting terror to allow myself to hope. I played all the usual games. *If the bus comes in the next ten minutes, I'll get into the grammar school.* My relationship with Christianity had been rather on-and-off, depending on whether a certain boy turned up at Sunday School, but for those weeks it was definitely *on* whether he appeared or not. I confided in the religious lady who taught me the piano (I was no good but she was encouraging and kind) and she made me kneel down with her, below a sepia picture of Hope blindfolded on a globe, while she prayed for my success. Privately, I made several bargains with the Lord.

Whether I kept these bargains or not, I cannot now remember. I was standing in the doorway of the kitchen when the postman came. My mother ran to pick up the terrible brown envelope – and then held it out to me, not I think from courtesy, but because she couldn't bear to open it herself. It wasn't the first time in my life I had been afraid, but I believe it was the first time I had been afraid for someone else and it is a fear that haunts me still. I can put up with my own disappointments; it is other people's that I cannot bear.

It was all right. I had my grammar school place. There were other ways out of poverty in the East End of London – boxing, or becoming an Olympic swimmer like Betty Slade, or a film star like my father's boyhood friend, Victor McLaglen – but the educational ladder was the obvious one for my mother to choose for her children. Her relief was beautiful to see. One child, at least, was safe for the time being. She hugged me, and asked me what I would like as a special treat. I said – I don't know why, perhaps because I had just seen the advertisement outside the local cinema – that I would like to go and see the women wrestling in mud, on Sunday, at the Odeon.

Naturally, like all really interesting treats, this was denied me. I never got to see the cheetahs racing at the Romford Greyhound Stadium either. Instead we went to Epping Forest for a picnic and it rained.

The uniform for girls at Ilford County High School was maroon and navy; maroon blazer and hatband, navy gym slip and white blouse. Although I begged my mother to buy my blouses at the shop where we bought the other things, she insisted that my grandmother should make them for me, out of cream Viyella, and that I should also wear Chilprufe knicker linings and vests that buttoned at the neck. I feared this fussy kit would expose me to ridicule, if not actual physical danger like the daily clean handkerchief at the elementary school, but except for the hateful babyish vests (which were not revealed until we had to change for gym) all the girls in my class were in a similar plight, their gym slips, hats and blazers bought with generous allowances for rapid and dramatic growth so that here and there a skirt brushed knobby ankles or a hat rested on a nose.

Not much could be done about the hats. People whose sleeves were too long were told to wear Cellophane cuff-protectors. The correct length for gym slips was more important. We were told to kneel. Those girls whose skirts fell on the floor were given notes to take home to their mothers. Jean and I, and other people whose skirts swung clear, were measured. An inch above the knee was the school rule.

Jean and I both passed this test. I was even praised for my blouse. The teacher said, 'A beautiful fit', and when I said my grandmother was a dressmaker, she called me a lucky girl. It was the first time anyone outside my family had suggested to me that a garment made to measure might be superior to one bought in a shop. I passed the teacher's praise on to my grandmother that evening, and even managed to apologise for having been so grumpy during the fittings. She gave one of her snorts and said, 'Oh, it's always what you don't have you value most.'

I was happy at this school from the beginning. All our teachers seemed to assume that we were as interested to learn as they were to teach, and they were astonishingly friendly towards us, as if we were people like themselves instead of members of an alien and hostile race. This was an unnerving change from the elementary school and it took some getting used to. I can remember watching these calm and strangely smiling grown-ups warily; half expecting them suddenly to turn black with rage and start to scream abuse, or beat me round the head with an ebony ruler, which had been the regular practice of one especially frightening teacher at the elementary school, a woman with a sarcastic tongue and a violent temper. (She died of cancer suddenly and none of us was sorry.)

My mother said, 'Why shouldn't they be nice? It's easy in a grammar school, they've picked the plums to teach. If you'd had your way and gone to the secondary, you'd have seen a difference in the teachers, I can tell you. Not their fault, either, no one can make bricks without straw.'

(After the war, in the fifties, my mother went back to teaching, in a new secondary modern school in Kent, and was appalled. The staff despised the children who had been weeded out by the eleven-plus, the same process of selection she had been so keen on when it applied to me. My mother said she was ashamed of her profession, and thereafter became a moderately ardent supporter of comprehensive schools.)

No one bullied me to work. No one seemed to notice that I fell into a trance in Algebra. I was excused Music because I could only sing in a goblin drone, and was allowed to spend those periods lying on my stomach in the library reading Chesterton and H.G.Wells and learning about sex in *The Science of Life*, a huge book written by Julian

Huxley with H.G. and G.P. Wells. If I could have thought up a way of getting out of games and gym I would have done, but nothing except a note from your mother to say you had a heavy period rescued you from that particular misery and my mother was of a mind that open air and healthy exercise was the best way to dispose of menstrual cramps.

We were a lucky generation. A lot of our teachers were the childless spinsters of the First World War; women in their forties and fifties whose unused, creative fire had been channelled into teaching little girls. Among these excellent women was an English teacher who was able to communicate the glorious excitement she still felt herself when she read a poem or a play, a Latin teacher who could make me understand that the prose style of Tacitus was a wonder of rhythm and economy, and Miss Clark, a History mistress who was a member of the Fabian Society and determined that as well as understanding the Chartist movement and the Congress of Vienna, the girls she taught should be alive to what was going on around them.

As a result, it seemed that I was more aware that war was coming than my mother. The daily newspaper she took was the *Daily Express* and as far as I remember it took an unrealistically sanguine view of Adolf Hitler's plans for Europe. My mother was unimpressed by my arguments that we should go to war to save the Jews, but on the other hand she gave more than she could easily afford to our school fund which paid for several Jewish girls to come to England, to be clothed and fed and educated at our school.

One of these refugees was in our class and I was deeply envious, both of the family that took her in, and of the girl herself, partly because she was pretty and clever, but chiefly because it seemed to me that her sad situation was sophisticated and glamorous, just like a Hollywood film. I didn't go to the cinema very often but when I did I totally suspended disbelief. There was a film star called Lupe Velez whom my Aunt Bridget especially admired and thought I looked a little like. I had never seen this actress in a film but Bridget gave me a photograph of her, cut from a movie magazine, and I spent hours dampening my hair and trying to brush it as straight as it would go, so that it would fall on one side of my face and make me look like her. Unfortunately, my hair was too light and curly when it dried, and to keep even an approximation of the sweeping-curtain effect I wanted, I had to hold my neck at an awkward, sideways angle, like the owner of the chow dog in our street. This became quite painful, but I persisted for several days, until my mother pointed out that if I were to meet the poor cripple in the street he might think I was mocking him.

Our Jewish girl had the same softly wistful look as the film star, Norma Shearer. We didn't know what had happened to her family and our class had been told before she came that we mustn't pester her with questions, but as a mixture of Norma Shearer and herself, she played endless parts in the stories I told myself about her, unreeling them before my inward eye in black and white.

Our refugee was a romantic figure to us all. There were several home-grown Jewish girls in our class, most of whom passed for Christian, attending morning assembly and Scripture classes, and there was no obvious anti-Semitism in our school. There was, however, one girl who didn't come to sing hymns in assembly with the rest of us and she *was* tormented – sneered at for her big nose, her greasy hair, her general otherness – and years later, when the full horror of the Nazi crimes were known, I remember feeling shocked and guilty when I recalled how we had treated her. But there had been another girl who suffered worse, and since she wore a crucifix on a gold chain, the only kind of jewellery we were allowed at school, she was presumably Anglican or Roman. This girl had braces on her teeth that made her spit; we thought it funny to surround her in the playground and taunt her, slobbering saliva and dribbling it down our chins in horrid imitation. She didn't cry, just stood there, back against the wall, her pale blue, protuberant eyes seeming to bulge beneath her forehead making her look even uglier than usual; squat, and scarcely human. It wasn't race or religion that made her or the Jewish girl a victim, but inadequacy and ugliness; we were rounding on the weaker members of the pack.

This was our first year at the grammar school, the year we were eleven, turning twelve. Later, we became more civilised – or perhaps only more subtle and discreet. But it was the last time I remember this kind of group persecution taking place. Perhaps the coming war was encouraging us to grow out of the tribal savagery of childhood a little earlier; great events working like growth hormones in the air.

In the playground, giggling conversations about sex began to replace hopscotch, headstands and skipping games, as well as ritual teasing. At thirteen, most of us were ignorant of everything except the basic facts of reproduction – how babies were born was easier for mothers and spinster teachers to explain than how they were conceived. Girls with brothers knew what a penis looked like, but no one who took part in these discussions had a brother old enough (or willing) to provide the really useful information we were looking for. Fathers were kept out of it; a certain delicacy, or gentility, prevented us from mentioning our parents in this context.

One morning assembly, after prayers, the headmistress, Miss Ethel Bull, an old Somervillian with hair cut in what was called an Eton crop, made an announcement. She knew that some of us were in the habit of walking to Ilford railway station through Cranbrook Park, the park next to the school. The police had telephoned to say they had had complaints about a man lurking there, upsetting women, and until they caught him all girls from the grammar school should keep away. This was a serious matter, Miss Bull said, and we must pay attention. The police were unwilling to alarm people unnecessarily, and this man was dangerous. From now on, until she told us otherwise, the park was absolutely out of bounds. It was a much longer walk to the station by the road, but there were buses, and the school secretary had been told to provide the bus fare from the petty cash to anyone who asked for it. Those who had specific trains to catch must be sure to catch the bus or their mothers might be worried.

The excitement took over morning school. 'Can't we go through the park if we go two or three together?' we asked our class teacher. 'I can't go on the bus, it makes me sick.' 'I dropped my pencil case yesterday, I wanted to see if the park keeper had found it.' 'Mummy usually meets me halfway, by the lake.'

'Mummy' would be told, apparently. A policeman was to be posted by each gate. I suppose this should have warned me but it didn't; the idea that the police were actually on the alert merely added spice to my intention. Of course I was going through the park. Why ever not? I always did. I could look after myself. Grown-ups always made a fuss about nothing. How was one ever to learn anything? I didn't care if no one came with me!

No one did come. (Jean must have been ill and away from school that day; she might have tried to stop me, but she would never have let me go alone.) I couldn't go into the park by the gate because there was a policeman there, but it was easy enough to slither under the railings from the school playing field; a forbidden practice, naturally, but there were several places where wriggling bodies had worn deep trenches in the earth.

I had to hang around a bit because the staffroom overlooked the field, and by the time I set off across the park the air was blue with dusk. No one was about, not even a park keeper or a dog, and I realised that I had counted on there being other people walking there. Too late to turn back, though; there was a darkish wooded area between me and the nearest gate. I tightened the straps of my satchel to make it sit higher on my shoulders, like a rucksack, and marched across a large expanse of open green towards the lake, the tennis courts, and beyond them, the main gate. I cleared my throat loudly from time to time, for comfort; I would have whistled if I could, but although my mother could whistle beautifully, not only a tune but a really shrill, boy's whistle, with two fingers in her mouth, I couldn't whistle any more than I could sing.

There was a little clump of trees in the middle of the open green; as I approached it one of the trees moved, detached itself. He was wearing an overcoat pushed back behind his elbows and he was playing with his penis. I couldn't see him very clearly, it was much too dark, but he seemed to have no trousers on. He said, in a completely kind and gentle voice, 'What do you know about this, little girl?'

I stood, it seemed for hours, quite still. Then choked, and ran. I think he ran after me; that is, I thought I heard his feet, but it could have been my own heart thumping, or my satchel banging on my back.

I can't remember if there was a policeman at the main gate of the park. I missed the usual train, two stops from Ilford, Seven Kings, then Goodmayes, and caught a bus instead; getting off at the pub, the Lord Napier, and running home.

My mother said, 'Oh, there you are! Isn't it dark today? Robin and I went to the fishmonger's and we looked for you coming off the train. I suppose you caught the next one.'

My heart began to thump again. I said, 'I came by bus. Miss Bull said we mustn't go through the park today, there was some stupid *man* hanging about and frightening people, so I caught the bus outside the school and came home all the way. It didn't seem worth getting off at Ilford Station. What's for tea?'

Chamberlain came back from Munich, waving a silly piece of paper. Miss Clark talked about appeasement, and her face was grave. She had had a thyroid operation on her neck when she was younger, and when she was especially excited or distressed, her stout neck reddened and the scar stood out, white and lumpy. Like her, I was disappointed that there was to be no war, but for different reasons. I was restless. I had recently begun to feel tamed and constricted. I had lost interest in the only social activity available, the occasional country rambles organised by the youth fellowship at the local church and although I had been an ardent Brownie to begin with, I had grown out of it long before I was old enough to be a Guide. I felt I understood my mother's boredom with our dull suburban life. Even if she hadn't pointed out to me that it was dull, I think I would have known by now that the grass was greener elsewhere; that there was a better life, where people lived in beautiful houses and had interesting conversations and adventures. (I had read about this life in books; reading, which is supposed to enlarge the mind was, by this time, increasing my discontent.)

The year turned. It was clear that peace in our time was an old man's delusion. Plans to evacuate children from the cities filled me with anticipation. I didn't want to leave home, or at least, I said I didn't to my mother, but in fact, deep down, the prospect thrilled me. A dazzling future beckoned. I saw myself living in a big house in the country with rich and educated and even titled people who drove about in beautiful old cars, always ate with candles on the table, fell in and out of love with each other, and generally had a wonderfully exciting life like the people in the Dornford Yates novels I had just become addicted to.

Although I didn't acknowledge it, I think I partly knew that it was time that my mother and I were separated for a while. I loved her passionately, but I was convinced she loved my brothers more than me and she often told me I was 'difficult'. She said I had got into the bad habit of saying things that nice people only thought; if I wasn't careful, this would make me unpopular. I guessed she was right. In every way, I despaired of pleasing her. Sometimes I despaired of myself. Besides apparently saying the wrong things all the time, I thought I was ugly; too short and too fat. Living in someone else's house I would be a different person; tactful, thin and pretty. I wrote a tear-jerking piece about the sadness of a wartime child torn from her loving family which, to my gratification, was published (though not paid for) in the local newspaper, the *Ilford Recorder*, but my true feelings were quite other.

Our school was evacuated a few days before war was declared. We were allowed to take two things with us, a small suitcase, light enough to carry, and a gas mask. We were given luggage labels with our names and addresses written on them to thread through our blazer buttonhole. I angered a normally indulgent teacher with what seemed to me a perfectly sensible complaint. 'It's *silly* for me to wear a label. I'm not luggage, and I'm not a baby. I should have thought I was quite old enough to know where I live and who I am!'

She said, 'Oh, Nina!' in a despairing wail. Then snapped, 'If this train is bombed, as it may very well be, that label might help some unfortunate air-raid warden to identify your body. If you're killed, don't you think your mother would be glad to know?'

That was a remark that could be taken more unkindly than she meant it. I was prepared to tell her so but she had sensibly moved on, along the crocodile of labelled children lined up on the station platform, ticking off surnames as she went. Jean, and her sister, Sheila, were in front of me, two girls called Pert, behind. (The older Pert was tall as a giraffe and moved a little like one; long neck swaying slightly forward as she loped along.)

We went to Ipswich, in Suffolk. My hopes of moving up the social scale through a lucky placement came to nothing. I was billeted on a family who lived in a council house and were definitely 'common'. On the credit side, however, they had a nineteen-year-old son who had just joined the Army and was busy polishing his boots and belt and brasses and indulgently, he invited me to help him.

The weather was glorious that September. My kind family, anxious that I should not miss my mother and my brothers, took me out for drives in their small car and stuffed me full of sweet biscuits, cakes and chocolate. If I was lonely though, it was not for my family, but for Jean. We had promised each other that we would stay together but the billeting officer had placed her and her younger sister with the local Methodist minister who had indented for two Methodist girls. I thought this was religious prejudice and shouldn't be allowed, but could find no one to say this to, so kept it to myself.

There was another girl billeted with me; a girl from another class, a girl I didn't know. All I remember about her was that she began to menstruate the first night we were there and that she thought there was something wrong with her. We were sharing a bed. I woke to find her weeping and the sheet all bloody. She said, 'Something awful's happened, I'm bleeding from inside, I think I'm going to die.' I thought she was pretending. *Of course* her mother must have told her! When I understood how ignorant she was, I did my best to explain as *my* mother had explained to me, but it was ages before she would – or could – believe me. And we were both equally appalled about the sheet. We crept into the tiny bathroom, washed the blood away under the cold tap, and put it back on the bed. In the morning it was stiff, but dry. I thought it looked as if one of us had peed the bed but when I said we should own up and say what had really happened, she began to cry with shame and I promised to say nothing.

That was the day the war began. We sat in the garden drinking fizzy lemonade and worrying about the sheet, and heard the Prime

Minister say we were at war with Germany. This council estate was built at the edge of the town; there was a ditch at the bottom of the garden, and a little wood beyond the ditch. When Chamberlain had finished speaking an air-raid siren sounded, and when the wailing died away the birds in the wood began to sing.

CHAPTER THREE

─────────── ✦ ───────────

Other People's Lives

I n 1976 the BBC bought the television rights of *Carrie's War*, my
novel about two children who had been evacuated to South Wales
during the Second World War. Looking for a suitable outdoor location, one of the production team came up with the coal-mining town
of Blaengarw.

Except in the coded way that most novelists make use of their lives,
cannibalising rough odds and ends of experience to make a tidy
whole, *Carrie's War* is not my story. But Blaengarw was the town where
some of us had been billeted for a week when our school was moved
from Suffolk to Wales. It was our first sight of a mining valley; the
black pit-head machinery, the smooth cones of the slag heaps dark
against the sheep-cropped green mountains, the narrow streets of terraced houses steeply climbing from the central main street like
bristles from a spine.

And for most of us it was our first real encounter with social injus-
tice. The mines in Blaengarw had been closed in the 1930s because
there was no profit in them; they were old, deep mines, dangerous to
work without new and expensive machines and safety equipment.
There was no other work for the miners; only a bit of light industry at
a bigger town down the railway line for their wives and their daughters. The week we arrived, in the spring of 1940, the money for the
necessary improvements had suddenly been found, the pits had been
opened, and the town was *en fête*. It was as if we had tumbled into a

festival, a carnival, an explosion of joy. There was no feeling in Blaengarw that week that we were at the beginning of a long, draining war. To this valley, the war meant work at last; life and dignity.

I stayed with a miner who was going down the pit the next Monday for the first time for seven years. He was a small, quick, bony man with a plump, smiling wife and a plump and beautiful daughter. There was a happy ease between them. We walked on the mountain, drank cold, sweet water from a spring, and went home to a kitchen that smelled of baking bread. Jean's parents came to see us and these hospitable people opened a tin of peaches, a rare treat at that time, for their tea. I wished I could have stayed with this happy family for ever and at the end of that short week I cried when I left them, as I hadn't cried leaving my mother and brothers in London. But most of the girls in my school had been sent to Aberdare, the town that is called the Queen of the Valleys, where there were both enough billets and a big grammar school building which we were to share. That some of us had been sent to Blaengarw instead had been an administrative mistake.

I hadn't deliberately, thirty years later, set my wartime book in Blaengarw. Or not consciously, anyway. All the same, when I was told that much of the film would be made there, it was as if a piece of a jigsaw had fallen into place. Blaengarw was perfect, the BBC said. There were not many valley towns as narrow and remote. The pits had been closed again soon after the war was over, and the town had hardly changed since then. There was even an ancient grocer's shop that could be used without much alteration as the shop where the children were billeted on the terrible Councillor Evans and his meek, frightened sister. I said, to the young man, the production assistant who had been researching the locations, that I thought I knew the shop. I told him how astonishing it seemed to me that he had chosen this particular valley, this particular town. He said, modestly, that his work had been made easy by my description; my book had 'led him straight *there*, no doubt about it'.

I was flattered. But when I went for a few days to watch the company filming in Blaengarw I found myself a total stranger. I couldn't find my way around at all. I had no idea how to find the railway station, or the school where we had waited to be collected by our hosts after our arrival. I had thought I remembered the name of the street where I had been briefly billeted with the happy family. It was the very street where they were filming, but I didn't recognise it. That is, I didn't recognise it when I first saw it. It was only later on, when I was watching the rushes at the end of the first day that it seemed to me as if that street, with the chapel and the grocer's shop exactly where the director wanted them, conveniently adjacent to each other, must have been the one I had been 'really' thinking of all the time. Certainly, I could no longer summon up the other map, the one that I had in my mind when I was writing the story, or thinking about it afterwards. The film, the image – as with a photograph of someone who is dead, or absent – had dismissed the original, or imposed itself upon it like a palimpsest.

Time had passed, of course. Thirty years between the war and the moment I decided that it might be interesting to write about it. And in the writing, as always, memory had been overlaid by invention and invention by memory, like painting on an old canvas. Even so, it was puzzling. Which was the 'real' Blaengarw? The unknown town I had just returned to where I couldn't even find the railway station? Or the Blaengarw in the film Paul Stone was making: a location, a setting that had, rather eerily, expunged the place I must have remembered in order to describe it clearly enough to lead the film-makers 'straight there'.

In much the same way the young actress who played Carrie replaced the mental picture I had had of her before, driving out what had already become, admittedly, a somewhat protean figure. There had been a number of editions since the book had first been published, all with different cover illustrations, varying interpretations of a girl I had perhaps seen, originally, as myself.

Not that Carrie is me. She is both more anxious and more composed than I think I was in 1940. I can be fairly sure that some of her feelings about being away from home for the first time, sent to live with strangers, are ones that I remembered. I had a photograph of my mother with me. So do the children in *Carrie's War*, but they don't often look at it.

'It was a good likeness of their mother and she was smiling at them but she didn't belong here. Like their father . . . she belonged somewhere else. In a dream, in another life.'

Which is how it often felt. Mothers and fathers could be an embarrassment when they came to visit. In one billet in South Wales, our foster mother, Mrs Jones, was a sad, nervous woman, hopeless at just about everything. She cleaned the floors; that is, I know she tried to clean the floors because I saw her on her hands and knees on the stone flags of the kitchen with a bucket of water and a scrubbing brush, but huge, glossy black beetles scuttled into the corners if you opened a cupboard. She shrank woollen clothes when she washed them – and she refused to let us wash our own things because she said it would make her 'look stupid' in front of the neighbours. Her idea of a festive meal was tinned pilchards, heated until lukewarm in the oven and served straight from the tin, and her conversation was limited to gruesome descriptions of the liver disease that had killed her only daughter, and her own operation for cancer. Her stomach was like a pincushion from the radium needles, she said.

When my mother came to spend twenty-four hours with me (a long, tiring, cross-country journey from where she was living by then), I was so anxious to protect my poor foster mother from what I imagined would be my real mother's withering contempt for her obvious inadequacies that I spent most of the precious time singing her praises. I didn't tell my mother that there were nights when our foster father would walk round the house in his nightshirt, carrying a guttering candle, and stand for some time, silently, beside the bed where we lay, eyes closed, feigning sleep. ('Mr Jones sometimes goes mad at the turn of the moon,' Mrs Jones had explained, early on. 'All his family are the same way. His brother hanged himself behind the kitchen door when the moon was full; he was big and heavy and it took several men to push the door open. But there's no need to worry about Mr Jones, he has his funny habits at that time of the month, so you just take no notice.')

This was my fifth billet and I was accustomed by then to other people's funny habits. In August 1939, leaving London on the train to

Ipswich, I had been alight with excited anticipation and I had not been disappointed. Life in other people's homes was always interesting if not always comfortable; you might have to eat Mrs Jones's food, but Mr Jones (a sweet man in his wits) was an adventure.

Most accounts of wartime evacuation concentrate on the shocking arrival in middle-class homes of hordes of slum children from cities like London and Liverpool with head lice and no table manners. Our experience, on the whole, was the other way around. One result of the separation of sheep and goats that took place at the scholarship was that most of the girls in my grammar school came from families that were slightly more prosperous and better educated than the average, which meant that some of them were bound to end up in poorer houses than they had been used to. One girl was so shocked by finding that the only lavatory was at the bottom of a cottage garden that she went back to London at the end of the first week.

I wasn't fussy about outside lavatories. I had spent holidays in Swaffham with my grandmother whose house had no inside sanitation, only a privy full of spiders that backed on to the privy of the house next door; usefully sharing the plumbing, but causing distress to sensitive people like a neighbour of my grandmother's called Miss Mantripp. She was a retired lady's maid and her opinion of outside lavatories was notable. 'It is most upsetting to a refined person. People sitting back to back. *Back to back and no relation!'*

What I found strange about most of the households I lived in between 1939 and 1942 was that there were either very few books or none at all. At home, my mother's own somewhat idiosyncratic collection ranged from *The Wandering Jew* to *The Man-eating Tigers of Rudrapriag* and *Precious Bane* but the bookcase in the living room also held all Dickens and Scott and Shakespeare, and other books that had belonged to her father. To find a living room without books was not only strange but even a little alarming; what did these people do for pleasure? Did they only read in bed? But there were no books in the bedrooms, either.

In the house where I spent the first winter of the war they played bridge instead of reading. My first billet turned out to be too far from the Ipswich grammar school that my school was to share and Auntie Beryl, bustling down to check on her daughters who were staying with the Methodist minister, set herself to finding me a closer one. She suggested to the minister that he should find suitable foster parents for me among his congregation and (I suspect) kept at him with her sweet, insistent smile until he did so.

I was instructed to call these foster parents Auntie and Uncle. I had begun to resent addressing people who were not my relations in this way but refrained from saying so when Auntie Beryl took me to meet them. I was awed by the comfort of their house, which was carpeted and cushioned to a degree I had never seen before; even the walls were covered with some sort of soft material with a plushy sheen. I thought it was a bit like a padded cell but I didn't say that either; living in other people's homes you learn to keep your feelings and opinions to yourself. And your doubtful jokes as well.

Like their house, they were a comfortable couple; well-fed chins and cheeks and solidly upholstered bodies. They had not planned to take an evacuee. They were taking me to please the minister. I was made to feel fortunate, and I did feel fortunate. I had a pretty bedroom; it was too cold to do my homework in, but a place was left clear for me at the end of the table in the warm kitchen. They were affectionate to me, and kind. They never left me alone in the house (I was frightened of being alone), and they left the landing light on for me at night (I was frightened of the dark). They always took me with them when they went out to play bridge and if I fell asleep going home in the car, Auntie would wrap an edge of her musquash coat round me. It was my first contact with fur and I was surprised by its weight and stiffness. And its not unpleasant fusty smell.

My mother came to see me. Auntie gave her a good tea, homemade jam and several kinds of cake, and when my mother thanked her, and said how good the cakes were, Auntie smiled and said she was glad my mother had enjoyed them. It must be a comfort to her to know that Nina would want for nothing, although of course she must know how expensive it was to feed a growing girl.

The government paid foster parents a small weekly sum; it varied between under ten shillings and seventeen shillings, depending on the age of the child. None of the women in the other families I was to live with in the future ever suggested it was not enough. This auntie, much the richest of them all, asked my mother for an extra contribution, a demand which I found shaming at the time (fearing it meant Auntie thought I had an unnaturally gargantuan appetite) and am shocked by now. I don't remember how much my mother paid her. She never told me. I think she was embarrassed by the request and by her own acceding to it, seeing it as craven. As I walked her to the station she said, 'I told her Daddy was in the Navy, on North Sea patrol.' Meaning, I suppose, that since neither Auntie's husband nor her son were in the Forces, she should have been glad to do whatever patriotic duty came her way without expecting to be paid for it. I didn't think Auntie would have realised my mother was rebuking her; she was not a subtle woman. I could have suggested a more telling thing to say, but didn't want my mother to think I was complaining.

At home, no more had been expected of me than had been expected of my brothers; we kept our rooms tidy, that was all. My mother disapproved of women who treated their boys like princes and their girls like skivvies. In Auntie's house, I washed enough dishes and did enough housework to more than pay for my keep, even at the lowly rates domestic servants were paid then. The worst job was washing the handkerchiefs that the son of the house, a theology student, sent home from college. He must have had a permanently heavy cold. As I was told to do, I scraped the slimy snot off his handkerchiefs with salt and a scrubbing brush, boiled them, and then scrubbed again. I suppose I could have refused but it didn't occur to me that refusing was a possibility.

I had no sense at all of what was expected of me, that was the trouble. At school our teachers told us to be 'good', to 'behave well to our foster parents', to 'help in the house'. If we felt something was wrong in our billets, or that too much was being asked of us, we must not complain to them as we might have done to our real parents, but come to tell our teachers.

What was *too much*? What was *something wrong*? I hated washing dirty handkerchiefs. But perhaps my mother had spoiled me. I could just see someone saying so. Raised eyebrows and a little smile. 'What a fuss about a bit of washing! When these good people have taken you in! I'm afraid you must have been spoiled at home, Nina.'

I was clearer about what was meant by wrong. But the amorous assaults from both Uncle and his grown-up student son when he came home from college were too shaming to report. Uncle would come up behind me when I was standing at the sink (washing dishes, scrubbing handkerchiefs), and put his arms around me. He squeezed my breasts quite painfully and wriggled his stomach against my back and bottom. I could see his pink and sweaty face in the spotted kitchen mirror that hung above the sink but I never met his eyes, nor gave any indication that I was aware of his presence. It didn't happen often, nor last long, and to ignore it seemed the simplest way of dealing with something that was about on a level of disgust with snotty handkerchiefs. The son, of course, was nearer my age, and up to a point I was prepared to be co-operative; when that point was reached I was big and strong enough to fend him off. In both cases I was more embarrassed than alarmed. My only real concern was that Auntie might come in. I knew she would be bound to blame me.

I didn't want trouble. I was happy most of the time, and quite fond of Auntie and Uncle, as they seemed fond of me. I spent Christmas with them, and my birthday in January, and they gave me *How Green Was My Valley* as a present, the hugely popular bestseller about South Wales, which was what I had asked for, because it sounded a little like *Tess of the D'Urbervilles*, as beautifully and richly sad. It gave me several happy hours, sobbing on my bed, and much, much more. It was, although I couldn't possibly have known it, a pointer to a whole new future; a kind of preparation for Blaengarw, for the mining valleys, for a sentimental attachment and a political allegiance that has informed my life.

Our headmistress enjoyed a touch of drama. After morning assembly she waited until she had our full attention, before she made her important announcement. 'This morning, the Germans invaded the Low Countries. Suffolk is no longer safe. So we are leaving Ipswich for the West.'

She claimed not to know exactly where we were going. Without saying so, she managed to give the impression that if the Germans found out our destination, national security would be endangered and Hitler would be bound to win the war. We left that afternoon. We must have changed trains in London, but all I genuinely remember about that journey (leaving aside my own fictions, or things I have been told) is the darkening landscape before the blinds were pulled down on the carriage windows; the blue lighting that was too dim to read by; the endless speculation, and the curious mixture of grinding boredom and intense excitement. During the early part of the night, a section of the train became mysteriously detached and sent to Blaengarw. By the time the administrative mistake had been discovered and put right, and Jean and I arrived in Aberdare a week later, most of the billets had already gone. That was my impression, anyway. We hung around the school hall waiting to be 'chosen' much longer than we had expected to. Perhaps the shortage of families willing to welcome us had something to do with our age: girls of fourteen and fifteen are more trouble than either smaller girls, or than girls of sixteen and over who might be thought able to look after themselves. It was certainly clear (clear to me, at any rate) that the town worthies who had come to look us over were avoiding Jean and me and others in our class in favour of bewitching little creatures with ringlets, or tall young women in the upper school, with shining page-boy bobs and shapely breasts.

Jean and I were billeted together in the end. Her sister went elsewhere, for reasons that escape me now. Scraping the barrel of prospective foster parents, we were taken home by a family who hardly seemed human to us. (The fact that adolescents often affect, defensively, to find most adults wildly funny, if not barking mad, may well explain why people tended to avoid us.) But they *were* odd, all the same, this family: half a dozen of mixed gender but the same size and shape – roughly cuboid and not much more than four feet tall. They all had permanent catarrh, breathing heavily through open mouths, and a strange gait that came from walking with their feet placed about a yard apart as if they had a barrel placed between their thighs. They were suspicious of the outside world, fastening the front door with chains and bolts and several powerful locks, and their eating habits were equally reclusive. Not only did we never eat with them; we never saw them eat or drink. There was an L-shaped living room and we were fed at a table in one side of the L, the side furthest from the kitchen, with at least two of the females always waiting on us; putting our plates before us and then retreating round the corner out of sight, until some sixth sense told them we had finished that course and they could bring our pudding. When our meal was over, we were sent to our room – presumably so that the family could indulge their secret feeding rituals in peace.

We were treated like princesses – and like prisoners. When we came back to our fortress after afternoon school, someone would always be waiting at the front door to let us in. As soon as we were in the hall, the door was locked and bolted. The relief the family obviously felt once this was done – the drawbridge safely up, the world shut out – was almost palpable. We felt it, and it affected us. We never went out after tea – not because it was openly forbidden, but because an inhibition that was almost fear had warned us not to ask.

We were physically quite comfortable. There was an inside lavatory and a proper bathroom. We were not expected to enter the L-shaped living room except for meals, but the heavily furnished and lace-curtained front room, or parlour, was given over to us for our exclusive use from Monday afternoon to Saturday morning, when it was comprehensively cleaned in preparation for Sunday. On Sundays the family sat there between meals and excursions to the chapel they belonged to, and we were banished to our bedroom. One Sunday we were lying on our beds, screeching with laughter over a pile of ancient women's magazines we had found in the wardrobe, when one of the males came thumping up the stairs. He growled through the door, 'That is not a nice noise for a Sunday.' He lurched downstairs again and we subsided, red-faced, rolling our eyes at each other, pretending we found this very funny, but we were really mortified.

We didn't complain to our teachers. There was nothing to complain about – except that we seemed to be living with people from another planet. And that was a minute discomfort compared with what other people were having to endure. To say 'there's a war on' was often put forward as an excuse for quite unrelated deprivations and had become a joke, but its personal references were not so risible. My father's armed merchant cruiser, Corfu, was in the North Sea. Her sister ship, Rawalpindi, had been sunk by the Scharnhorst and Gneisenau, and German submarines were hounding the Atlantic convoys like packs of wolves. And my mother, five-year-old Robin, and Jean's parents were living through the London blitz; their letters, fleshing out the news, told of a friend's house bombed, whole families dead, the city burning.

Our teachers were more perspicacious than we thought. One came to call on us a Monday evening after school. We listened from the parlour and heard the rattle, creak and groan as chains were removed, bolts drawn, heavy keys turned in solid locks. The whole business took about four minutes – we had often timed it, waiting outside on the doorstep – and when the door was open and we were reluctantly summoned to meet our visitor, we thought she must be ill, her face had gone so pale. She muttered something about checking whether we were coming to some evening event or other – nothing that we had heard of, but since we had abandoned any idea of going out after lock-up we may not have listened to the announcement in assembly – and glanced beyond us at one of our custodians, lurking in the hall. I started to say – or whisper, rather – that I was sorry we couldn't ask her in, but then it occurred to me that she was too scared in any case. It was a novel thought to have about a teacher. I gave her a foolish, conspirator's grin as she smiled distractedly and backed away.

She was the youngest of the staff; this was her first teaching post. It was a much older teacher who interviewed us the next day, inviting us into the staffroom and giving us cups of tea and biscuits before she began to question us. I thought they all seemed rather silly and trivial things to fuss about – the separate meals, the locked front door, the Sunday isolation – but the teacher's expression grew solemn as she listened.

She shook her head at last and said, 'It's lucky there were two of you together. It might have been a third-former on her own!'

We were moved the next morning. Another teacher came with the billeting officer and spoke to our hosts in the parlour while we packed our things. The blood burned in my face as I descended and saw three of the family waiting in the hall; standing mute, bewildered. It felt like the worst, the cruellest thing that I had ever done. We went out and heard them lock the door behind us, first the locks, and then the chains, and then the bolts.

I said, 'It wasn't so bad, really. I mean, they were quite nice.'

'Not really suitable,' the billeting officer said briskly. She tapped her forehead with her forefinger. 'Harmless, you know, but not much up there.'

Our new billet was above a chemist's shop. The chemist and his wife were childless. They had asked for a girl on her own, hoping for someone who would be a daughter to them. They had taken the two of us reluctantly but we didn't understand that until later. When we arrived they were welcoming to both of us.

The chemist's wife had magnificent red hair which reached to her knees when it was loose. She looked wonderfully romantic in the mornings, going to the bathroom in her white Viyella nightdress with her crimped and shimmering hair floating around her like a cloak. Dressed, and with her hair braided round her head, she was just a portly woman, too young to be so fat, or 'comfortable', as her husband kindly called her. Both of them ate five serious meals a day. Breakfast was bacon and eggs and tea and toast and home-made marmalade. Elevenses were coffee, cake and biscuits, and a ham sandwich if anyone was feeling especially faint with hunger. Lunch was three courses, all substantial: soup, meat, vegetables and pudding or dessert. High tea was eggs, salads, bread and butter, Welsh cakes, pikelets, muffins – and the cold ham always on the sideboard if anyone felt extra peckish. Supper was a lighter meal so as not to load the stomach too heavily before the night: just cheese and biscuits, sweet and plain, a fruit flan, perhaps, a plate of leftovers from the earlier meals which it would be a shame to waste, and big mugs of steaming chocolate, or Ovaltine, or a choice of several other kinds of malted milk; the chemist stocked a wide range in his shop and he liked to taste them all. Curiously, this was the only billet where I sometimes crept into the larder to steal food. Once, in the middle of the night, finding myself awake and inexplicably hungry, I dropped a tin of biscuits in the kitchen and was terrified – absurdly, because if I had been discovered my hosts would simply have blamed themselves for not providing sandwiches and a thermos of hot milk beside my bed.

An ENSA theatre company came to tour the valleys and the cast were put up in private homes in Aberdare. The actress Sybil Thorndike and her husband, Lewis Casson, stayed with our chemist and his wife; Sybil was playing in *Medea*. Jean and I were given free front-row tickets but all I can honestly recall about the performance was that the apron of the stage had been extended forward with some packing cases covered with planks and hessian and every time Sybil, who was a well-covered woman if not in quite the same league as the chemist's wife, leapt towards the audience with one of the dramatic howls her part demanded, there was enough ominous shifting and creaking to make us gasp and put our hands across our mouths.

Watching Sybil eat was as riveting as the play. I had heard of Lewis Casson, but *she* was a famous actress, a goddess in my theatre-loving family's pantheon. And there the goddess sat, at the chemist's groaning board, and tucked in like a starving navvy. She had very pale blue eyes. Most of the time they were fixed on some distant nothingness, as if no one around her was worth looking at, but when the rest of us had eaten to a standstill and she was reaching out her hand for another crumpet, those pale eyes fell on me. She said, 'You may well watch me, girl. This is the first decent meal I've had for weeks. If you are ever tempted to an actor's life, remember me.'

Except to ask her hostess (at the top of her clear, carrying voice, as if she didn't care who heard her) where she could wash and hang out her dirty knickers, this was all I heard Sybil Thorndike say off-stage. Her husband, Lewis Casson, was more sociable. After one supper that was even more gargantuan than usual in their honour, he sat beside the fire with Jean and me and talked to us; about the play, about literature and life in general. He didn't patronise us; he wasn't merely being 'nice'. He appeared to be genuinely interested in what we said. He asked me what I hoped to do and I said I wanted to write. This was actually a deadly secret but he seemed the sort of person one would naturally tell secrets to. He accepted this as if it was the most normal ambition in the world and it was the first time, I think, that I saw it could be possible for me.

We stayed a winter and a spring with the chemist and his wife. They did not want to be 'Auntie' and 'Uncle'. They told us to call them by their Christian names. This seemed not quite right to Jean and me and so we called them nothing; a tricky business to begin with but we learned to manage with coughs and smiles and various interrogatory cries.

They were especially kind to me at Christmas, when Jean went home to London and I stayed in Aberdare because my brother Robin was in hospital with diphtheria, but I think that as a pair we were a disappointment to them. We were their first evacuees; they were Jean's third set of foster parents and my fourth. They were innocents and we were old in this experience; a year in other people's houses had made us circumspect, cautious about how much of ourselves it was safe to offer. At Christmas, when I thought my baby brother might be dying, I was glad for the chemist's wife to hug and comfort me; delighted to be allowed to help the chemist in the shop. (Counting saccharines into packets of a hundred was a treat; they left a curious, unsweet sweetness on the fingertips.) But when Jean came back for the spring term I didn't need these kindly adults any longer; my friend and I together made a self-protective unit that must have seemed to them to rebuff their interest and affection.

The end was amicable. They made some face-saving excuse or other – needing the bedroom for the daughter of a friend in Birmingham is what I dimly remember. Jean and I were to 'pop in' whenever we wanted, and would always be welcome at meal times.

We never went back. Although there were days, staying with Mr and Mrs Jones, that we salivated at the thought of those substantial meals, when we passed by the chemist's shop we always crossed the road. I seem to recall seeing the chemist's wife somewhere or other, hand in hand with a pretty little girl. This may be no more than a tidy, novelist's imagination, but it was what she wanted, what she needed, and I like to think she found the daughter she was looking for.

Mr and Mrs Jones suited us much better. Mr Jones might have his monthly eccentricities but to bear them patiently was all either he or Mrs Jones ever really asked of us. He worked so hard down the mine, sometimes doing two shifts in twenty-four hours, that once he had scoured off the coal dust (standing naked in the zinc bath in front of the range fire while Jean and I ate our tea in the corner of the room) he had no energy left for much more than sitting in his wheelback chair beside the fire. And she, mourning her only daughter, dead at seventeen, had no thought that someone else's girl could ever take her place. For us the sense of not being watched, *brooded over* by concerned adults, whether they were our own parents, or foster parents wistfully looking for a loving intimacy, was an amazing liberation.

We were not only free from emotional tensions, but free in more practical ways. Our school shared a local school building, using it alternate mornings and afternoons, holding the out-of-school lessons in various church halls and Welsh Nonconformist chapels. The distances between these makeshift classrooms meant that it was easy to get 'lost' between Ebenezer and Elijah – I did Latin in one, History in another. If more of us turned up to our classes than might have been expected, this may have been because we were a biddable generation, or simply that there was little alternative amusement on offer.

We bicycled over the Brecon Beacons, on borrowed bikes with my brother and his friend. My mother, fearing Peter would not pass the scholarship had sent him, at eleven, to a boarding-school for the sons of merchant seamen. According to him, this was an appalling institution, a Dotheboys Hall. He ran away repeatedly, and eventually my mother talked the educational authorities into allowing him to join Ilford Grammar School for Boys which was also in Aberdare, because I was already living there. Peter was billeted about half a mile from me, a pleasant walk along the abandoned railway line behind the Joneses' house. His foster father was an architect, his foster mother eager to mother him because he was a pretty boy, and he was happy to be mothered after the rough treatment at the Merchant Navy school. The only disadvantage to this excellent billet was that every Friday night the architect went out alone and came home maudlin drunk. He would stumble up the stairs to sit on the edge of Peter's bed and weep. He scattered his loose change, sixpences and shillings, sometimes as much as several pounds, upon my brother's pillow. 'I'm a worm,' he would sob. 'Take the worm's money. That's all worms are good for.'

Although I thought Peter should have returned the money, he thought differently, stashing it frugally away in his Post Office savings book. He said his foster mother had told him it was a fair wage for putting up with her silly husband's weekly nonsense. He had fantasies of amassing a fortune, but he didn't stay with the architect long enough. My mother, who had taught in London throughout the Blitz until Robin caught diphtheria, moved out of London to a farmhouse on the borders of Shropshire and Montgomeryshire, the Marches of Wales, and enrolled both her sons in local schools. I put up a plea to join them but it was only half-hearted. I liked my school, and was sensible enough to see that I was getting an unusually privileged education; because so many girls had drifted back to London, those of us who stayed behind were getting, in the musty, dusty chapels of Nonconformist Wales, almost individual tuition. And it was the best teachers who had stayed in Aberdare; the dedicated women, the widows of the First World War.

I was unwilling to give up my freedom, too. As long as we were home by ten at night, Mrs Jones never asked where we were going. If we thought we might be later than ten, Mr Jones would come and meet us; from a friend's house, a cinema, a musical evening with the headmistress, a political meeting. He would wait patiently and inconspicuously until we appeared and then lope home beside us, a silent, shadowy bodyguard.

I had discovered politics, a headier excitement in Wales than anywhere else in the United Kingdom. I heard Aneurin Bevan speak in Merthyr Tydfil, in the valley next to ours, and walked back over the mountain with an excited group of boys and girls – I was not the only

London evacuee to be politicised by Wales. Miss Clark held weekly evenings in the house she had rented with another teacher; coffee and sandwiches followed by discussions in which we all were expected to take part: 'The Social Consequences of Food Rationing', 'The Mediating Roles of Principle and Expediency in Government', 'Class in British Society and its Effect on the Economy,' 'The Future of Farm Subsidies' . . .

Sometimes, to startle us into being a little less solemn, Miss Clark would start up a hare to test us. Once, she suggested that in a good society everyone would share the dirty, boring jobs: teachers, surgeons, politicians would take their turn at picking up the rubbish. Daringly, I asked her if she meant that dustmen would be allowed to take their turn at being surgeons, and she nodded approvingly. She said something like, 'All visionary speculation can lead to absurdity', and although we didn't altogether understand her, we all laughed. At the end of one of these meetings she gave me *The Ragged Trousered Philanthropist* to read.

It was clear to me that the miners of South Wales had been wickedly exploited by the mine owners. When Mr Jones, that good man, heaving himself out of his wheelback chair to go off for an extra shift, spoke simply of 'doing his bit' for his country, I allowed myself the pleasure of righteous indignation. What had his country done for him? Or for Mrs Jones? An exhausting, laborious, dirty job? An ugly, inconvenient house with no proper heating except a huge range fire in the kitchen which had to be kept blazing summer and winter because there was no other way to cook, or heat the water. Just to keep the place clean was unremitting labour! Mrs Jones let me help her only once. There was a slag heap behind the house, on the far side of the old railway line, and when it rained the slurry from its surface streamed down the mountain; liquid coal, like lava. I came home one afternoon in a heavy storm, and found her trying to sweep the sticky slurry out of the kitchen door with an ordinary kitchen broom. I got a shovel and a wheelbarrow from the tool shed and cleared up the worst of it; I would have finished the job and scrubbed the floor, if she had not hung on to my arm, preventing me. I said, 'Don't be silly, you sit down. When I've done, I'll make you a cup of tea.' But she was crying, tears of desperation. 'It's not right you should do this kind of dirty work. It's not a job for an educated girl.'

We had exams that summer; the London Matriculation Board. They worried Mrs Jones more than they worried us. She said she wasn't sure our health would stand the strain. We did our revision, sitting on slippery leather chairs at the polished table in the cold front room – cold, even on the warmest summer's day. She tiptoed in at frequent intervals with cups of strong, sweet tea. And in the mornings, she added wizened bacon to our usual breakfast of tea and blackened toast.

The summer holidays came and we went home. Jean to London; I to join my mother and my brothers in the farmhouse. We packed all our things as we were told to do in case the families we lived with should want to use our rooms, but we were comfortably certain, as we said goodbye to Mr and Mrs Jones, that we would see them in the autumn. Jean had left before me and they took me to the station; Mrs Jones unfamiliar without her enveloping, flowered apron, Mr Jones wearing his best jacket and his Sunday cap. I had a lump in my throat; they were suddenly so dear to me. I hung out of the window dangerously, waving until the train went round the bend and took me out of sight. I had no idea that it was the last time I would see them. No idea that I had already, without meaning to, betrayed them.

My mother had rented one enormous room in a big old farmhouse that had seen better days. The room had a modern bathroom attached to it that the farmer's wife had installed, but no running water. There was no mains water supply, and to bring water uphill from the brook would have been a more expensive business than the rent for the room would justify. So we carried water pumped up from the well in the farmyard, used the bath for storage and the earth closet at the bottom of the vegetable garden for sanitary purposes. It was an airy little house with three holes of different sizes cut in its scrubbed, wooden seat. A sociable lavatory, my mother called it and we three children thought this very witty.

The only electricity came from a generator in the barn that lit the cow shed and ran the new milking machines; inside the house we moved about with candles and ate meals in the soft light of a hanging oil lamp that threw mysterious shadows on the walls and ceiling. The old house was beautiful, with enormous rooms, some of them big enough to turn a horse and cart in; broad, dark oak floorboards polished to a velvet shine; a warren of empty attics for children to play in; a 'secret' cupboard stair and a cool, stone-flagged dairy where the farmer's wife hung hams and made salty country butter – a golden treat at a time when so much food was rationed.

And not only butter. There were eggs and milk and chickens on the farm, and the occasional, illegally slaughtered, pig. (The pig-killing always took place at night when the squealing echoed round the hills, proclaiming what was happening for miles around, and the next morning the policeman would pedal up the lane and hang about the yard, making conversation until the farmer's wife produced a shoulder or a leg of pork for his wife to cook for Sunday dinner.) During the war, no one in our part of the country went shooting or fishing for sport. Instead, the farmers spread a barrier of sacks soaked in petrol on the River Severn, setting them alight so that all they had to do was wade among the trapped salmon and gaff them with sharp kitchen knives. And everyone shot pheasants, which were so plentiful in the woods that it was said (although I never saw it done) that the simplest way to catch them was to make them drunk with raisins soaked in brandy and then knock them on the head.

My mother was about forty and a pretty woman. The local farmers were mostly Welsh, and deeply shy. They brought her tribute, a brace of pheasant, a whole salmon, a pair of fine, fat rabbits, and left it for her on the dry stone wall. They would make a clatter in the yard and when she came to her window they would grin and blush and be off before she could come downstairs to thank them. Perversely, the only thing my brothers really wanted was corned beef, in tins.

I had a lovely summer, helping with the harvest, and doing all the country things I had read about in books – collecting eggs, fetching the cows to be milked, picking whimberries on the Long Mynd, the long, crouching mountain we could see from the window of my mother's room. She made whimberry tarts and we ate them with thick, yellow cream until we were tight as drums. I said something about cherishing the memory of meals like this next term when I was facing a tin of pilchards and a stale slice of bread and margarine at Mrs Jones's table.

'You're not going back *there*,' my mother said. And then, 'Didn't you know, Nina?'

I was sure I hadn't known. And yet I can remember the bitter taste in my mouth. The taste of guilt. I must have exploded with anger because I can hear my mother saying calmly, 'Don't wave your arms about like that, you remind me of Hitler. And you were the one who wrote about how awful the food was, you said you were often *hungry*. Did you expect me not to pass it on?'

I must have written to her. Oh, I know I did. But I had meant to joke, not make complaints. I tried to write funny letters home, just as I acted the clown sometimes in class, making outrageous or provocative remarks. My stomach, stuffed with cream and whimberries, turned to lead inside me. How often had I mocked poor Mrs Jones, made fun of her to amuse my family, my friends, my teachers?

My mother said, reproachfully, 'I talked to Jean's mother on the telephone.'

The nearest telephone was a public box halfway up the Long Mynd, a half-hour's stiff climb away. Whatever I had written, my mother had been sufficiently alarmed to set off up the mountain on an expedition she would normally only contemplate in an emergency, or to telephone my father at a prearranged time when he was docked in Liverpool.

'We both wrote to Miss Bull,' my mother said. 'Really, Nina, if you've made this up she will be very angry.'

Which was worse? To be a liar, or a sneaky traitor? I fancied neither role. 'Can't no one in this family take a joke?' I groaned – and slouched off to the hay loft which was a good refuge for hurt feelings; dusty, warm and peaceful with the old Hereford bull stamping and chomping in his stall below.

Our new foster mother's husband was in the Army. She had one child: a fiendish little girl who ate all our butter ration. This auntie was obsessively house-proud. We were not allowed to go upstairs more than twice a day in case our great, galumphing feet should wear out the new stair carpet. The bathroom was upstairs. Our natural functions were not always obedient to the house rule and she had sharp ears. However softly we crept upstairs, she would rush out of the kitchen, to the hall and back again, round and round like a demented ferret in a cage, muttering her mantra, 'Up and down, back and for, in and out, messing and humbugging about, wearing out the carpet.' Her other choice remark was, 'Remember the little niceties of life!' (This was chanted at us if we sneezed before we could find a handkerchief, or hung our knickers on the washing line the right way up so that they looked like knickers and might inflame the man next door.)

She was a healthy, rosy woman, with big, shining eyes that rolled and showed a lot of white as if she were a horse. She wasn't Welsh; she came from somewhere in the Midlands. Her food was adequate but dull. Hot water on Shredded Wheat for breakfast to 'soften' it and therefore use less milk. Roast meat on Sundays, cold on Mondays, 'done-down' – minced, and mixed with Bisto gravy – Tuesdays, Wednesdays and Thursdays; Fridays and Saturdays various gastronomic treats peculiar to Wales, among them, faggots, a dark, solid, cake-like mixture of entrails which was nicer than it sounds.

She had a sister living near, whose husband was also in the Army and who had the same rolling, horse's eyes. Sometimes she would come to fetch our foster mother to go out for the evening, and before they left they would tease us about our ignorance of sex. They affected to find it comic that girls our age could still be virgins. I think this teasing was not meant unpleasantly or spitefully, only as a kind of ritual warm-up for a merry evening of flirtatious dalliance in the pub, but we found it embarrassing. I remember saying, stiffly, that we were not ignorant, merely inexperienced. I thought this was an unanswerable put-down but it only made them giggle wildly, like two silly girls. We were glad to see them go even though it meant we were left to babysit and the child was a monster of a kind neither of us had met before. She hated us – which was fair enough: she must have sensed we hated her. She refused to eat her supper, clean her teeth, or go to bed. On one occasion she threw a carving knife that missed Jean by a whisker.

This was our last billet, our last 'auntie'. We were in the first year of the sixth form and there were not many of us left in Aberdare. Girls had gone home for the holidays, and stayed. The school in Ilford had been kept open with a skeleton staff but by now there were more girls there than here.

Except for a few of the youngest girls who stayed on with their Welsh families and transferred to local schools, we all went back to London. My mother was settled in her farmhouse, there was no question of her returning to the house in Goodmayes, and so I went to stay with Jean, which pleased us both.

The Blitz was over but there were land-mines and flying bombs. The school was full of sandbags and there were bomb sites everywhere. The tennis courts in the park had been torn up by a stick of bombs, making the game more interesting than I had found it before, or have found it since. During the Blitz my mother and Robin had spent nights in an Anderson shelter in the garden; Jean's family had a Morrison shelter in the house. Jean's father slept with his head in the cupboard under the stairs: being a brainy man, this was the part of his body he cherished most. The Morrison shelter was in the dining room where once, long ago, Jean and I had sat to do our homework and sort used postage stamps. It was a kind of stout, strengthened table. Jean and I slept beneath it and her grandmother slept beside us. We lay and listened to the doodle-bugs droning overhead. We hoped they wouldn't stop, not just because the unmanned flying bomb might fall on us but because that marked the moment when Jean's grandmother would throw herself across us, shielding us with her stout little body. She never seemed to sleep and she was heavy.

I was curiously unafraid. There was even an exquisite excitement sometimes, listening to the engines of death above me. If I were to write about living in a city under siege, I would be able to describe the sharpened sense that danger gave to ordinary life; the exhilaration of having survived the night, the bomb, the mine, but it would seem crudely insensitive to write about someone who was not in the least *afraid.* I was afraid of lots of things; the dentist, being alone in a house (listening for a clicking latch, a creaking stair) – but I was not afraid of bombs. Of course emotions fade from memory, or sometimes, if remembered, seem unbelievable after a lapse of years. Did I, did *she*, feel that? How can it be?

I had no one to be responsible for, of course. I was at the age when death seems unimaginable. And there were more important things to think about, like passing examinations and falling in love.

I was always falling in love. I had fallen in love in Aberdare with a boy called Coker from the boys' school who once carried my satchel for me up the steep hill to the chapel where I had my History lessons. I fell in love with the men on the farm where my mother was living; especially with the son who was my age, and with the succession of young, dark-eyed, Italian prisoners of war who lived in the farmhouse. It was love at a distance; except for the farmer's son, who was more playmate than lover, I don't think any of the objects of my passion noticed me. I didn't mind. I loved so much at that time, with an energetic, all-embracing love. I loved the farm. I loved the bare Welsh hills. I loved A.E.Housman; I rode over the bare hills on the farmer's black pony and shouted his poems aloud.

It was harder falling in love in London. After Coker, I told myself I was no longer interested in boys, and most young men were away in the Forces. There was the youngish man who had run the youth fellowship at the Anglican church, and who lived a few doors away from Jean's family, but he was, Uncle Hedley said, 'a confirmed bachelor'. I said I supposed that was because he lived with his mother and had to look after her, and Uncle Hedley chose not to enlighten me. In desperation I managed to fall in love with the manager of the Woolworth store where I did a Saturday job but it was a fleeting affair, ending when I discovered that he had told his assistants they must not sit down on the seats behind the counters while on duty. As most of them were middle-aged or old with bunions and varicose veins, this was real hardship. I had not been taught by Miss Clark for nothing. I cannot remember now which Shop Act it was that the manager was disobeying but at that time I had that sort of information at my fingertips. I accosted him during my tea break (so that I should not appear to be skiving off when I should be working) and gave him chapter and verse. He listened politely and said this was something he didn't know about but since I was still at school and learning about that sort of thing he was sure I must be right.

To my gratified astonishment, he walked round the store, stopping at every counter and instructing the women that, as long as they were not actually serving a customer, they could sit down when they felt they needed to. I was flushed with my success but I didn't get the praise I expected. 'You're just here Saturdays, aren't you?' one woman said – giving me a kind but weary smile. Although I didn't need to ask Uncle Hedley what that meant, I told him all the same: I had a shocked suspicion that he was not as firmly on the side of downtrodden workers as he should have been. He listened, and he sighed.

I had not intended to go to university. My dream had been to work on a newspaper and be a war correspondent. Uncle Hedley pointed out that the war would be over by the time I was trained. Auntie Beryl said I ought to go to Oxford, and since she had a way of achieving what she had set her mind to, I found myself sitting the entrance exam in a secluded classroom with one other girl, an invigilator, and a pile of white paper in front of me, without being altogether certain how I had got to this point in my life.

I can only remember one question that I answered. It was in the General Paper; we were asked to choose from a list of titles and write an essay. I chose 'The Future of Farm Subsidies'. Although I don't know which of Miss Clark's lines of argument I took, or exactly what I wrote, I know I wrote it passionately; my fountain pen flew most satisfactorily over the paper and I had a fight to finish before the clock struck the hour.

I had a letter offering me an interview. I went to Oxford in my school uniform: navy gym slip, maroon blazer and hat. I had been growing, I had nothing else that fitted me, and was ashamed when I arrived at Somerville and found that the other girls waiting outside the Principal's room were wearing what I thought of as 'best' clothes: plaid Gor-ray skirts and velvet-collared jackets. The pitch of their voices and a kind of expensive glossiness about their hair and skin made them seem like healthy young mares. They all seemed to know each other, they all came from private boarding-schools, and as soon as I heard them and saw them I knew it had been presumptuous folly to imagine I might be allowed to join this exclusive society. While the girls chattered breathlessly on I stared proudly ahead and smiled secretly, deciding that if one of them spoke to me I would pretend to be a Jewish refugee and answer in a foreign accent.

I was the last on the list that morning. The other girls went into the Principal's room one by one, and, when their interviews were over, clung to each other. 'Oh my *dear*,' they wailed, 'wasn't she *terrifying*? Of course we haven't an *earthly*.'

I was more intimidated by them than by the prospect of meeting the gorgon who clearly lay in wait for me in the study. I knocked and went in. Helen Darbishire rose from her chair by the fire and held out both hands. She said, 'Come in, dear child. I have been looking forward to meeting you.'

For a second I thought there must be someone else in the room for those superior girls to have been so alarmed, but there was only this small, rosy woman, beaming at me with a grandmotherly air. We sat by the fire and she asked me about my school, my family, the farm where my mother was living, and what I hoped to do 'after Oxford'. I said (timidly) that I wanted to write and (rather more confidently) that I intended to do something to make our country a better place to live in once the war was over. I told her what it had been like in Wales between the wars: the unemployment in the valleys, the miners with silicosis, the children with rickets. I feared as I spoke that my indignation sounded naive but she listened with an interested expression as I unfolded my master plan to set the world to rights and, when I had finished, it seemed only polite to show interest in her in return. I asked, what was her special subject? She told me her great love was Wordsworth. I said I had read him, 'of course', but found him indigestible. Too wordy, I said, too sentimental. And all that romantic tosh about Nature! Helen Darbishire, the great Wordsworth scholar, heard me out patiently. She said I should try reading him again in a year or two and I might find I felt differently: the age at which one 'came to' a poet was very important. She smiled and gave me a chocolate. She said, 'Dear child, we will be happy to have you and I believe you will be happy with us.'

I didn't get an exhibition but I was pleased I had a place. It meant the local educational authority would give me a county major scholarship. But that alone would not be enough to send me to Oxford and my parents could not afford to help me. I would have to win a state scholarship as well as a county major, and state scholarships at that time were limited in number. To be sure of getting one, I would have to have at least three distinctions in the four subjects I was taking in my Higher School Certificate in June. And the prospect of that kind of success was something I could only dream about.

So I wasn't too distressed – or pretended not to be – when July came and went and I had not had my results. They were to be sent to us by post. Jean had received hers, and so had all the others in our class, but war had made the post unreliable, and it was not until towards the end of August that I abandoned hope.

I persuaded myself that I didn't greatly care. I might become a Land Girl. Or go into the WRNS. Or I could, at last, become a journalist. I thought I might write to the *Ilford Recorder* and remind them that they had published a piece I had sent them at the beginning of the war although I realised it was unlikely that a local newspaper would immediately give me a job as a war correspondent. If all else failed, I could marry a farmer. There were plenty of unmarried young farmers around.

I juggled these alternatives but did nothing about them. In the meantime, I helped with the harvest. I forced myself to like the cigarettes that were pressed on me by Billy Wilkins, the insurance agent who called on the farmer's wife once a month and taught me to smoke – Park Drive in the wainshed, out of sight of my mother. I learned to milk the cows. I cleaned out the cow sheds. I helped the farmer with his mournful-faced sheep that he maintained were more intelligent than folk gave them credit for. I liked the sheep well enough but I was fonder of the pigs; I thought it was a shame that they should be thought of as dirty animals.

I was cleaning out the pigsty when our regular postman came puffing up the lane on his tall old bicycle. I waved at him. I hadn't seen him for a while. He had a smallholding and there had been a temporary postman while he got his harvest in. He got off his bike, leaned it against the gatepost, and came into the yard. He had half a dozen letters in his hand. He said, 'Some of these will be a bit late, I found them at the bottom of my sack this morning. But they'll be mostly bills, I reckon, old brown envelopes the lot of them, so not much harm done.'

CHAPTER FOUR

A Box of Lucky Bricks

In the autumn of 1943, Oxford slept in a strange and timeless silence. No bells rang in wartime, from clock tower or steeple, and there was almost no traffic; the uncluttered curve of the High, the spires of the colleges, slept in the clean, moist, quiet air as in some old don's dream of peace.

Not that, coming from the Welsh Marches, it seemed quiet to me. There was only one tractor in our valley; on our farm, we ploughed and harrowed and harvested with two golden-coated shire horses. As I pushed my bike (laden with suitcases and Uncle Stanley's typewriter) from the railway station to Somerville, I felt that I had arrived at the hub of the universe.

I was not nervous. After meeting Helen Darbishire, how could I be? The tone of my interview with her still sang sweetly in my head; a note of courteous respect for callow opinions followed by a gentle suggestion that I might, perhaps, think again. This educational approach was doubly effective in wartime Oxford. There were so few undergraduates and, proportionately, so many dons that most tutorials were one-to-one: one student, one don.

Sometimes this concentrated exposure could be alarming. I had gone up to read French – for reasons which are now obscure to me since I had no gift for languages. My tutor was Enid Starkie, a small, sharp woman, reputed to be a lesbian, who wore splendid clothes in startlingly flamboyant colours; purple, pink and orange. She was not in the least like Helen Darbishire. I read her a long, pompous essay on Baudelaire that I had conscientiously paraphrased from all the best sources. She blazed at me with her astonishing eyes, like blue fire, and said, 'Tell me, Miss Mabey. Do you know anything *at all* about sex?

It was not altogether because of Miss Starkie that I changed schools to read Modern Greats. I knew enough French, I decided; to spend my time at Oxford just being taught to speak or read it better would be wasting time on a mere technical achievement. I wanted to learn something new.

I was sent to Lindsay, the Master of Balliol, to be taught Philosophy. This was meant as an honour for me, but it turned out a dismaying experience for both of us. He had not taught girls before, nor any student of either sex from a state grammar school, and could not believe I had never learned Greek. He seemed convinced (although he was far too polite ever to say so) that I must be concealing this simple and fundamental skill out of some mysterious modesty. He was very kind, comforted me with hot, milky drinks, and tried to explain about Bishop Berkeley. Unfortunately, what was so simple to him, the flowing order and clarity of his beautiful arguments, became, as it dripped through the sieve of my incomprehension, bewilderingly muddled and murky. I began to feel as if I stood on the threshold of a brightly lit room but a locked door barred my entry. I went to Helen Darbishire and asked if I might change my Philosophy tutor. I said I was too stupid for Lindsay. She laughed and kissed me and told me to tell him myself. When I managed to do so, stumbling and ashamed, he apologised (which made me feel worse) and sent me to Dr Mackinnon of Keble, a large, untidy, engaging man who rolled on the hearth rug and played with the coal in the scuttle, sometimes chewing a lump (with frustration, presumably) while I read him my essays.

One afternoon he said, when I had finished, 'What you have just told me, Miss Mabey, is profoundly true . . .'

I waited, holding my breath – had the door opened at last without my perceiving it? The fire hissed. Mackinnon sighed and shook his heavy head. '. . . And profoundly unilluminating.'

I said I was sorry. He offered me a sardine sandwich with his coaly fingers and I was brave enough to explain about the locked door. He gave a relieved shout of laughter. 'All you need is a key!'

He sent me to a pupil of his, a young don from Glasgow living in a bed-sitting-room in north Oxford who taught me, very slowly and patiently, the basic words, the first principles; coaxing me into the sea of philosophical method as one might coax and encourage a nervous swimmer until one day I realised, with detached surprise, that although I was out of my depth, my head was safe above water.

Ungrateful memory cannot supply that kind young man's name, nor the names of others who taught me. Only faces, voices, remain. There were two refugee European professors. One wrapped me in a rug (Oxford in wartime, in winter, was damply, bone-achingly cold) while he read Hobbes aloud in a Viennese accent, or flirted with me, saying I reminded him of a squirrel. 'You are so shy on the ground, but once safe in the tree you chatter and chatter.' The other, a whey-faced giant with large, dangling limbs that seemed only loosely connected to his vast frame, tried to persuade me that darning his socks would be a more suitable occupation for a young woman than learning statistics. He was also interested in the sort of man I would like to father my children; he was an expert on diverting a discussion on the Law of Supply and Demand to what he seemed to find a more gripping topic. And there was a small, gallant Englishman who had been parachuted into France to join the Resistance and who occupied our tutorial hours very pleasantly by telling me how interesting (though alarming, of course) his experiences had been, and showing me how to light fires without kindling, using neatly folded newspaper fans. I cannot remember what else he taught me, any more than I can remember the contents of the lectures I occasionally went to. All that comes back, try as I will, are small things. G.D.H.Cole's red carpet slippers. And Lord David Cecil's more neatly shod foot gyrating in circles, his sweet, elfin face wildly grimacing as he read a paper to a literary society I sometimes attended.

*

There were so many societies. Standing in front of the noticeboard my first term, I was dazzled by the delights that they all (with the exception of the Bell Ringers and the Rowing Club) seemed to offer. I had only to join this, or that, for a whole new world to open before me, a glittering world of agile and civilised argument, brilliant occasions at which I would shine and, most important of all, meet young men.

I longed for men in a way that was not consciously sexual, nor even romantic. Except for Jean, most of the girls at school had often laughed at me, sniggered at my 'odd' ideas and opinions. This had made me uncomfortable with my own sex and a first look round my fellow pupils at Somerville had not suggested I would fare any better at Oxford. Like the girls at school they seemed to fall into two distinct groups: the plain ones, with their damp, eager smiles, drooping skirts and wrinkled stockings, and the brilliant and self-sufficient young goddesses who were already, while I eyed them cautiously in the early days of that term, greeting each other in Hall and Common Room with confident affection and laughter. I did not want to be trapped by the first group and, though I would have roasted in Hell rather than lower myself to confess it, I feared that the second would never admit me to their exquisite company. Men, I told myself, would be easier to get on with, more tolerant, as well as being more interesting. Once I knew some young men everything else, the social and intellectual excitements I longed for, would automatically follow.

This approach had its pitfalls. By the time I discovered that some of the plain girls were amusing, not all the goddesses quite unapproachable, and that the ideas my schoolfriends had found so extraordinary were almost distressingly common at Oxford, I had spent a great deal of time doing things that secretly bored me, like watching rugger, or drinking beer, or discussing Wittgenstein. I joined the Welsh Nationalist Society chiefly because it was a proscribed organisation in wartime Oxford, but also in pursuit of a Welshman. I painted flats for the Experimental Theatre Club production of *The Dog Beneath the Skin* because I admired (from afar) a second-year medical student whose name was Keith Taylor. Although I had no real desire to join the Oxford Union – the standard of debate was so low, most of the speakers so deep in youthful self-love they made even me feel old and tired as I listened – I threw pamphlets and balloons from the public gallery in support of a motion to admit women because the president invited me to. That was Tony Pickford, a man whose frail, beaky good looks, style and intelligence seemed to me in my first year the only exemplar in the whole university of what I had expected Oxford to be; the fact that he was known to be dying from a rare blood disease gave him an added, and awesome, romantic attraction.

Tony was 'so mature', we said to each other at Somerville. Maturity was a quality we honoured deeply because most of us so conspicuously lacked it. We had come straight from school, our call-up deferred; the sprinkling of undergraduates over seventeen or eighteen in their first term were either, like poor, clever, doomed Tony, and later, Ken Tynan (clever but silly, we smug girls dubbed *him* at Somerville), unfit for the Services, or refugees from battle-torn Europe, or even older wars. There were several aristocratic and charming Chinese (with whom I eventually celebrated VJ night in London), one of whom claimed to have walked out of China across the Indian frontier 'disguised as a peasant'.

Our war barely touched us. It was there in the background but we had grown up with it and were used to it, grumbling on over our heads like so much dull adult conversation. In the vacations we worked on farms or in factories, and in the term, as well as fire-watching and manning the college stirrup-pump team, we were detailed to help the war effort for a fixed number of hours a week. Since my particular duty was listed as 'Entertaining American soldiers' I found it no hardship. All I ever did for those polite, bewildered young men, kicking their heels in the camps outside Oxford, was to invite them two at a time to tea in my room in Somerville and to serve as a waitress twice a week at the Red Cross Club in Beaumont Street. Although I knew other girls did more (it was clear that one Somervillian, who changed from her drab working clothes into butterfly garments made from home-dyed cheesecloth when she left college at six every evening, was not merely setting forth to cut sandwiches) an obscure prudishness stopped me admitting it. Fellow students gossiped and giggled. I maintained that if this girl was more generous with her time and her company than the rest of us, it was largely because she understood the Americans better. She was studying sixteenth-century English literature and it was well known that the American language was closer to Shakespearian than to modern English. It wasn't only a matter of accent but of the way words were used. When this argument was received with coarse laughter, I backed it up by quoting the Master of Balliol. *His* war work with our allies consisted of taking occasional Philosophy seminars and he had told me that he sometimes found communication difficult. A statement like, 'Well, I guess I swing along with Berkeley here,' was, he said, a fair example of how two nations could be divided by a common language.

We were divided by more than that. These Americans were new to war; pampered, peacetime children with smooth-milk-fed faces, whose fledgling innocence about the kind of minor privations we were accustomed to, amused, astonished and shocked us. Working at the Red Cross Club, we were often appalled by the amount of delectable food left on plates and casually thrown away.

Not that we were ever really hungry. We were rationed to two ounces of butter a week but college meals were adequate if dull, and cheaply supplemented by British Restaurants, by the Taj Mahal in the Turl where you could get a good lentil curry for ninepence and by the Cake Factory at the end of the Banbury Road. Since men and women were not allowed in each other's colleges before lunch or after six in the evening, tea was the meal to which we invited each other and the factory cakes were standard fare. Wholesome enough to begin with, they went stale very rapidly, and there were girls at Somerville who claimed to measure the strength of their host's affections by the freshness of the buns he offered them. If they were still moist, he cared enough to have risen early and bicycled to the factory before they had sold their ration of supplies for that day. However much he protested his passion, if his cakes had already acquired that familiar, desiccated texture, disintegrating dryly on the tongue, he could not be considered really 'serious'.

This kind of conjecture occupied a frivolous amount of our time and attention. Few of us were sexually experienced, although we often affected to be, out of pride, and we yearned for romantic love of a kind we had been taught to expect by the cinema. During the vacations we sometimes fire-watched in the university buildings (in return for bed and board in our colleges), and although I remember one eerily unpleasant week, spent in the museum, sleeping on a camp-bed between a hideous mummy in a glass case and a stuffed alligator, what chiefly comes back, when I recall the part I played in the defence of my city, is sitting on the roof of the Bodleian Library playing planchette with an upturned glass and a circle of letters, trying to coax from the Fates the colour of my true love's hair.

There must have been more important things to remember; actions, encounters, occasions. I remember VE night, the tumbling bells, the joyful streets full of people, but chiefly because I met an undergraduate at Carfax with whom I fell in love. And although I can, with an effort, remember being unhappy sometimes, crouched chilly and bored in my room waiting for something exciting to happen, what memory offers with ease are the happy times. A dance at Queen's (wearing a black taffeta dress I had bought second-hand for £5), swimming naked in the river with my friend, Mairi MacInnes, the poet; skating on Port Meadow when it flooded and froze one bitter January; the mysterious, pale beauty of the blacked-out colleges on clear, moonlit nights; evenings at the Playhouse, or the Classic Cinema in Walton Street where they always, invariably, seemed to be showing Hedy Lamarr in *L'Extase*. I remember the pleasure of my small, dull, box-like room where, for the first time, it seemed, I was able to be, or to become, anyway, the person I wanted to be without interference – or only interference of a kind that only protected my freedom. I never found the college rules irksome. To have to be back in Somerville by 11.15 was an excellent way of escaping, without appearing too unsophisticated, from unwanted sexual entanglements. For those who did not want to escape, there was a door into college from the Radcliffe Infirmary next door that was left open at night because the nursing staff had taken over one of our houses as a dormitory for the duration of the war. If this door was locked, for some unpredictable reason, there was always the high wall between the college and Walton Street. The only time I climbed it, I sat on the top and saw Helen Darbishire walking in the garden. She looked up and said, 'Who is that?' I was too frightened to answer. Helen had always been gentle with me, but she was not gentle with everyone. Already that term, she had sent two girls down – for idleness, I realised afterwards, but at the time I believed it was for climbing in after hours. But all she said was, 'Oh, it's only you, Nina. Do get down at once, child, and have a hot bath before going to bed. You might get a chill, sitting on that stone wall.'

It seemed, for a long time, that my affection for Somerville was centred almost entirely on the small, warm, dignified person of Helen Darbishire. Perhaps because my tutors were almost all men, and I had always found men easier to get on with than women, I found the dons in my own college remote, a little cold. And being shy of other girls, I was never much involved in the internal affairs of the college. Among my contemporaries the ones I remember, apart from close friends, are those whose paths crossed mine later, or who have achieved some kind of notoriety.

I remember Richard Burton partly for this obvious reason, but I would have remembered him anyway, for one strange, shared experience. He was an RAF cadet, up in my first year, on a two-term short course. I met him at a party; I was wearing a black dress my mother had made me out of some satin my father had brought home from China before the war and Richard said I looked 'very sophisticated'. We danced, neither of us very well, and he asked if he could pick me up the next day and take me out to tea.

He arrived late, limping dramatically. He had cut his foot, he announced, and was in terrible pain. I was only moderately sympathetic, and it amused me to observe that his limp disappeared as we left Somerville and walked to the tea shop in the Banbury Road. The shop was closed and we stood on the pavement, feeling hungry and cheated and looking, I imagine, disconsolate. A lady appeared from the house next door and said, 'Were you two young things wanting tea?' She was a small, bright, bony woman with an incisive, cultured voice. We smiled at her foolishly. She said, 'You poor children, how disappointing. Will you let me give you tea?'

She swept us into her house, up to a large, first-floor drawing room, full of rich clutter: pictures and books and beautiful carpets. We sat where she told us, on a silk-covered sofa in front of a leaping fire and eyed this grand room and each other awkwardly. She brought a huge, laden, silver tray and set it before us. She said she had to go out, to a lecture, but we could stay as long as we wanted, take our time over our tea, and just remember to close the front door firmly behind us when we had finished.

We were too amazed even to thank her – as I remember it, neither of us spoke a word. She vanished with a merry wave of her hand, a good fairy in this odd, Oxford pantomime; her heels clicked down the stairs, the door slammed.

Richard said, 'Do you really think she belongs here? I mean, suppose she's the maid?'

I said she wasn't a servant, you could tell by her accent; she was just kind and eccentric. But his doubts set my mind working. The tea was delicious; the scones home made and thick with butter, and the jam was real jam, in a pretty glass dish with a silver lid. While Richard talked about the part he was playing in Nevill Coghill's *Measure for Measure*, I wondered if our generous hostess might be a madwoman, given to inviting strangers in from the highways and byways and feeding them the family rations. Or worse – a cunning professional thief who had stolen a few priceless trinkets and was using us as a kind of camouflage screen, while she got safely away.

Richard asked me if I would like to spend a weekend with him in London. He knew Emlyn Williams, he said, and we could stay at his flat. I shook my head, laughing nervously. Even if I had believed he knew Emlyn Williams – and I was sure I could recognise a boastful lie when I heard it – I was far too preoccupied to consider this invitation seriously. As I ate greedily, I listened for the sound of a key in the door, a heavy step on the stair. Any minute now some large, angry man would burst in, accuse us of breaking and entering and telephone at once for the police. Of course they would realise we were innocent *finally*, but there would be a lot of unpleasantness first. And rightly so. We hadn't stolen anything, not intentionally, but we had eaten this tea – scones and jam and several ounces of butter. We would be humiliated, exposed as gluttons. I said I felt sick, and Richard agreed we should go. He seemed apprehensive himself suddenly, though his estimation of our hostess was more charitable than mine. He said, when we stood safe outside, 'She was very trusting, wasn't she? You'd have thought she'd be worried we'd walk off with the family silver.'

We only met a few times after that. He was too young for me, seventeen to my eighteen, and he had boils on the back of his neck. But years later, whenever I saw that coarsely pitted, middle-aged rake's face on the screen, what rang in my mind was that one, awed, boyish remark.

He is fixed in my memory at the age he was then, as Margaret Roberts (who was to become Margaret Thatcher) is still a plump, neat, solemn girl with rosy cheeks and fairish hair curled flat to her head who spoke as if she had just emerged from an elocution lesson. She and I came up the same term, both grammar school girls on state scholarships. Our first-year college photograph shows us standing side by side in the back row, but my only clear memory of her is, appropriately, of a political argument.

I think it was in the long vacation at the end of our first year and we were both fire-watching; thrown together by chance in the room of a third girl who was a friend of mine. This girl had a cold and was sitting with her head under a towel inhaling Friar's Balsam. Margaret and I argued over her shrouded head.

I was, by then, an enthusiastic, if undistinguished, member of the Labour Club. I was genuinely shocked to hear that Margaret had joined the Conservatives. I told her so. The world was changing, I said; to cling to the instinctive habit of deference towards 'top people' which was all, to my mind, she was doing by belonging to the Conservative Club, was not only old-fashioned but a clear dereliction of duty. She and I, with our lower middle-class backgrounds, had been lucky to get into Oxford. It would be despicable to use our good fortune simply to join the ranks of the privileged! Our duty was to make sure, when the war ended, that a new, happier, more generous society would take the place of the bad, old, selfish one.

I cannot remember how she replied initially – I was enjoying the sound of my own voice too much to pay much attention to hers – but sensing, perhaps, that my lofty sentiments were not having quite the missionary effect I had hoped for, I shifted my ground and pointed out that the Labour Club, besides being on the side of the angels, was also more fun. All the really lively and interesting people were members, Ernest Gellner, Michael McMullan, while all the people in the Conservative Club were dull as ditchwater.

Margaret smiled, her pretty china doll's smile. Of course, she admitted, the Labour Club was, just at the moment, more *fashionable* – a deadly word that immediately reduced my pretensions – but that, in a way, unintentionally suited her purposes. Unlike me, she was not 'playing' at politics. She meant to get into Parliament and there was more chance of being 'noticed' in the Conservative Club just because some of the members were a bit stodgy.

My friend raised her head from under the towel and said, 'You lost that round, Nina.'

Put down, I went away muttering. But if some of us in the Labour Club were playing at politics, by the next year we were playing in earnest. The whole Labour movement was riding on a high tide of hope, preparing for the election of 1945. A contingent of us went to Reading to campaign for Ian Mikardo and found ourselves caught up in an extraordinary atmosphere of political excitement that everyone seemed to share – soldiers on home leave, old men in pubs, tired women in bus queues. We canvassed until our feet were blistered and our throats were sore. I stood on a soap box on a street corner to speak about a free and equal society but everyone was talking and laughing and no one could hear me; then a man shouted, 'Let the lass have her say,' and I was struck dumb with terror and had to be rescued. We slept on the floor in Labour Party Hall and ate marmalade sandwiches, all we could afford, at the People's Pantry. We marched through the streets, singing, 'Vote, vote, vote for Mr Mikardo, chuck old Churchill in the sea.'

On election night, Mikardo gave a party for all the volunteers with whisky to drink but nothing to eat and everyone, I was told, got drunk. Everyone except me. I had to leave two days early to go home to the farm. I had promised to do the round for our postman while he got his harvest in.

I loved our valley; it was soft and rolling and so wide that you could see for miles. Below the window of our one enormous room, the chicken field sloped down to the brook that marked the boundary between Shropshire and Montgomeryshire, between England and Wales. The Mill House was beyond the brook, on rising land, and beyond the Mill House, at the end of the lane, Granny Evan's cottage and Frances Holloway's little shop on the main road between Churchstoke and Bishop's Castle. Higher, up the steep bank of the Long Mynd, you could see the farm where it was said the farmer shut his wife in the pigsty at night and drove the pigs up to the bedroom. (Hearing this apocryphal tale for the second time, about another farmer in a different part of the country, I began to doubt the truth of some of the other tales my grandmother had told me.)

I always hitch-hiked home with my bike and suitcase and typewriter. Long-distance drivers were the best bets; they were glad to have company and were less likely to make embarrassing propositions. ('Ten bob if you'll stop by the side of the road for half an hour,' was the usual euphemism. The first time I heard it I didn't understand what it meant and so found out, inadvertently, the most tactful way to turn down that sort of offer.)

Everyone hitched in wartime; the only person who ever suggested to me it might be a bad thing to do was an Admiral (well, he was in the Navy, glittered with gold on his uniform, and had an almost equally resplendent driver) who picked me up on Clee Hill above Ludlow and took me all the way to the end of the farm lane, holding my bike on the running board himself. He said, as he set me down, 'I've gone out of my way to see you safe. I've daughters of my own. Next term, make sure you put aside the money for your railway fare. Write to your mother if you haven't got it.'

I smiled at his innocence. I didn't feel poor, since we were all poor and shabby, neither poverty nor shabbiness troubled us, but after I had paid my battels at the beginning of the term I had £12 left over from my scholarship and the county major grant to last eight weeks and pay for books, and extra food, and fun. I could earn ninepence an hour in the vacations if I worked on one of the bigger farms near Bishop's Castle, but I preferred to help on our own farm where the only paid hand was Bill the cowman (a red-haired giant who had a laugh so loud it echoed round the valley and who only spoke in grunts and swear words) and the occasional Italian prisoner at harvest time.

I was a convert to country living, and like all converts, extra zealous. I begged the farmer to be given a fork and a pile of manure to spread; to be allowed to muck out the cowsheds and the pig styes. Cleaning out the privy was the pinnacle of my achievement in this area and, on this occasion, I was paid: the farmer, unable to credit that a townie would take up his light-hearted offer, had mentioned the huge sum of £5. He paid me punctiliously and took me more seriously afterwards, trusting me to drive a horse and harrow, to dip sheep, and, one wonderful, cold winter's night, got me out of bed to hold the lamp at a difficult birth. His arm was buried almost up to his shoulder inside the cow; he sweated and grunted as she threw him from side to side. He pulled until the tiny front hooves appeared, held together in his hand, and the calf was born in a slippery rush of mucus and blood. I said, when it had risen to its tottery feet, 'This is the best moment of my whole life.' And, instead of laughing at me, as the moment I had spoken I had feared he would, he said, 'I never get tired of it; it always gets me in the throat.'

We had an old battery wireless to which my mother listened faithfully, but the batteries were always running down and so the news of the war, of bombings and battles, and merchant ships sunk in the Atlantic, came to us very ghostly and faint, as if being transmitted from another world a long way away.

I listened with my mother sometimes, knowing she was terrified of hearing the name of my father's ship, but when I was there, the world of the farm absorbed me to the exclusion of everything else, even concern for my father, who spent the war at sea. Even to the exclusion of Oxford. On the farm Oxford vanished from my mind almost completely. It was as if the people I knew there had only a limited life; once I had reached the valley and started to push my bike up the lane, they began to lose solidity and dimension, fade into shadows, transparent, gossamer thin. And yet, during term time, the life of the farm was still with me, in my thoughts, in my mother's letters. In my mind, the farmer, his wife, his children, his neighbours, all our country friends and acquaintances, had a much more vivid and substantial existence than undergraduates and dons.

Perhaps they were more interesting to me because I found them more mysterious. I could guess at the thoughts and feelings of people at Oxford; what they cared about and how they lived. Even if some of them came from grander backgrounds than I did, I had read about their sort in books. Life in the Welsh border country seemed both more innocent, and darker. People worked hard physically and took an easy, unselfconscious pleasure in every social occasion; market day, the church whist drive, going to Shrewsbury on the bus, the Young Farmers' dance. On the other hand, I heard tales from my mother that chilled my blood.

There was the scandal of the fat Land Girl who lived with her mother in a village between the farm and Bishop's Castle. She went into labour entirely alone, late one night, and left her dead baby in a drawer when she went to work the next morning; her mother found it and ran screaming from the house, her wits disordered, never to recover. Worse, much worse, was the dreadful story of the two evacuees; two tiny boys who had been taken in by a hill farmer who had hoped for a pair of stout lads to help him round the farm. The children had been left at the farm by a billeting officer who fell ill and resigned soon after, and, through some administrative error, they were not transferred to the list of the person who had taken over. No one noticed when the boys did not appear at school. The farmer's wife fell ill with TB, which was common in the Marches at that time, and went into a sanatorium. A month later the little boys were found in the farmer's stable, dead of starvation, their arms around each other. There was a tin of dirty water beside them and a mouldy crust of bread.

This tale, relayed by my mother with a certain amount of morbid enthusiasm, obsessed me. I could not comprehend how such a thing had happened: this hill farmer, so people said, was just slow and stupid, not vicious or violent, not a monster. There was evidence that he had cared for the children to begin with in a rough and ready way, and that one, or both of them, had fallen ill; filthy sheets were found in the bedroom they had shared, and perhaps that was why he locked them in the stable. He may not have intended them to starve to death, he gave them bread and water, but perhaps from that time on, as they deteriorated, they seemed less and less real to him; creatures of no account, useless animals, not human any longer.

My mother said, 'So you think it's all right to ill-treat animals, starve them to death?'

I said I was only trying to understand how such a terrible thing could happen, and she snorted with disgust. 'Typical of you to stick up for a murderer!'

I told myself that it was impossible to have a rational conversation with my mother. I asked her, meekly, who had found the children. 'Oh,' she said, 'didn't you know? It was our postman. When you did his round last winter you must have delivered to that farm.'

It was Easter now. Our postman had gone to visit his daughter in Swansea for a week after Christmas, and I had taken on his round as a trial run: he had hinted (no one in that part of the country ever committed themselves, it was all done with nods and becks and wreathed smiles) that if all went well I could take it on for two weeks in the summer.

I felt cold and dizzy, as if some giant hand had picked me up and dropped me from a height. I couldn't place the farm. I couldn't bear to ask my mother where it was. I had borrowed the farmer's black pony to do the round at Easter. Had I tied the pony to the gate and walked to the house to deliver the letter, or (as I usually did if there was a dog loose, the hill farmers' dogs were often savage) pushed the gate open and ridden across the yard, my legs tucked up, out of reach? *Had the children been there then, dying in the stable?*

I said, 'I probably didn't have any letters for him. I only did the post round for a week. Most of those hill farmers, they don't get much but bills. He said, the postman said, just to shove them under a stone, they never pay anyway, till they get the red warning.'

*

There were no meaty scandals attached to our farmer's family, only ordinary, real-life drama. My mother became a close friend of the farmer's wife; a sparky Welsh woman, small-boned, quick-moving, with a pretty cat's face and very pale skin. She looked like Vivien Leigh. The farmer was older and slower and quieter and a little sad. He used to sit, in shirt-sleeves and jerkin, in the big kitchen by the light of a single oil lamp, staring into the range fire as if weighed down by some secret sorrow. It made him seem romantic to me and I often sought him out to talk to; although he never said much in reply, he seemed to accept my chatter and my company and, on occasion, called on me to help him. There was the night I helped him with the cow. And the night of the German invasion.

The farmhouse had once been a monastery; later on, a gentleman's country house when it had been given its name, Owlbury Hall. There had been a grand oak staircase carved with owls, but both staircase and owls, we were told, had been sold to the United States when times were hard in the 1920s. Now, though beautiful to our eyes, it was shabby and run down; in the attics, you could see the sky through the roof and, although the oak floors gleamed like satin on the middle floor, there were several large rooms that stood empty, unfurnished, unused except to store apples. I slept in one, on a camp-bed, and from time to time the farmer's wife would let a room, in return for help round the farm and in the dairy, but no one stayed long.

The Brights, Mr and Mrs Bright, were the only tenants I ever saw. They moved, with a great deal of vast furniture, into one of the rooms on the ground floor that, as long as I had known it, had been uninhabited except by mice. They were vast people, like their furniture, and Mrs Bright was so completely square behind that it looked to us as if she had a box tied on beneath her clothes. We decided, after much awed speculation, that it must be a kind of orthopaedic garment, or a corset of an exceptionally strange design.

The night of the German invasion, my mother woke me. 'Go and look out of my front window,' she said. 'Don't make a noise. I'm waking the others.'

The window looked on to the yard and the lane. The moon was clouded and there was a steady drizzle. There were two big trucks parked inside the yard gate. About a dozen men, wearing heavy sacks over their shoulders to protect them from the rain, were moving about in the yard, a couple of them up the big tree just inside the gate, looping wires over the branches – setting up some sort of radio, Peter said, in a whisper. Everyone, everything, was misty and grey.

The farmer and his wife appeared in my mother's room. And Mr and Mrs Bright. Mrs Bright was wearing a pink-and-white flowered nightgown with nothing underneath. I knew, because as she came in, carrying a small oil lamp, I had seen the dark stubs of her nipples poking through the thin fabric and, lower down, the shadow of her pubic hair. My mother made her turn off the lamp and Peter and I made way for the Brights at the window. Peter began rolling his eyes and jabbing with his finger. I looked where he pointed. Mrs Bright's bottom, stuck out as she leaned over the windowsill, was still square as a box. It even had distinct angles. 'Go on,' Peter whispered. It was the only chance we would ever have to find out for certain. I could stumble against her; in the excitement, she might not notice if my hand were to brush against her by chance . . .

My mother whispered, 'The church bells will ring if there is an invasion. Could we hear Lydham church from here?'

The farmer said, to me, 'Come on Nina, better find out, no sense standing here.'

I put on one of the old raincoats that hung behind the door and followed him down the stairs. In the big kitchen, he picked up the guns, the twelve-bore and the shotgun. He gave me the shotgun and pushed open the door. He said, with a ghost of a chuckle, 'You go on, you've got an education, you speak foreign languages.'

This was an old joke between us. 'Busy at your lessons again?' he would say when he saw me with one of the Italian prisoners in the orchard or the wainshed. But most of what they tried to teach me had to do with love. Nothing, even if it had been the right language, that would help me to treat with a German invader.

I advanced, heart in mouth, the shotgun tucked under my right armpit, the barrel waving uncertainly in front of me. I had no idea how to aim it, let alone fire it. Behind me, the farmer chuckled again. Go on, he said. 'Go on, now. Challenge them.'

I croaked. 'Who are you? What are you doing?'

And realised, before anyone answered me, what the farmer had clearly known earlier, that these sinister sack-shrouded persons were not enemy aliens dropped from the sky, but the local Home Guard out on an exercise. 'Dirty night for it,' my farmer said, and the officer who appeared to be in charge (retired regular Army and local landed gentry) grunted agreement, looking wistfully at the farmhouse. Round the edges of the blackout in the kitchen window, a warm red glow beckoned. The range fire, damped down at night, would burn until morning.

The farmer seemed lost in thought for a moment. Then he said, 'Yes. Well if you don't mind I'll be off to my bed. Early start in the morning.'

'The cheek of it,' my mother said when we went back upstairs to tell everyone they were safe for the moment, the Home Guard was standing watch. 'Expecting to be offered a hot drink in the warm when they've just terrified us all out of our wits!'

'No need to be frit,' my farmer friend said. 'Nina here would have seen them off. Where's Aby now? Sleep through the crack of doom that lad would.'

'He puts in a long day's work for a boy,' my mother said, with mild reproach. She didn't say *unlike Nina* but to my jealous and suspicious mind – ever on the lookout for an imagined slight from her – that was what she meant; contrasting my easy life with Aby's hard one. Aby was seventeen or eighteen now. He had left school at fourteen to help his father on the farm, and although such a cutting short of education was truly shocking to my mother, she frequently implied, perversely, and when it suited her, that it was somehow to Aby's credit. People who sacrificed themselves, gave up, did without, were always morally superior in my mother's view to people like me who did what they wanted, 'had things their own way'.

'Aby's not a boy, he's eighteen,' I protested childishly. But she wasn't listening. She was watching the farmer's wife who was looking, suddenly, paler than ever; white as chalk. She gave a soft, exhausted moan and would have fallen if my mother had not been there to catch her.

The farmer's wife was dying. She told me herself while I was helping her feed the baby chickens in the orchard. 'They said they took it all away but it seems they were wrong. They never know, do they? I don't know how I'd manage without your mother here. Father doesn't know, nor Aby yet. Though I don't know what they thought I was doing in the old hospital! Just some women's trouble, I expect.'

She was so frail, when she came to our room to see my mother in the evening and stretched out her thin hands to the fire, her fingers looked almost transparent; you could see the flames through them. She and my mother talked about clothes rationing. My brothers were growing so fast, and Aby was 'desperate hard' on his boots. Sometimes gypsies came to the farm, selling clothing coupons. My mother said that when they next came she would be glad to buy some.

They were silent a minute. Then the farmer's wife said, 'Will I have to give coupons for my shroud?'

She sounded entirely matter-of-fact; she might still have been discussing Aby's boots. My mother took her small, pale hands between her larger ones and said, 'I think it might be a good idea if Nina made us all a cup of tea.'

The coming summer was to be our last summer on the farm. My mother was going back to London in the autumn. The European war was over; her sons needed further education, Peter in engineering, Robin in a better school. And there was a housekeeper downstairs, looking after Aby's younger sister, and reigning over the big kitchen where we had always been so welcome. Now we entered the house through the back door and, if we wanted Aby, waited outside in the wainshed till he came.

Some days I did the post round on my bicycle; other days, when there was a bigger postbag, I took the farmer's pony. I picked up the mail as well as delivered it and carried stamps to sell and a hand-held machine for weighing parcels. The parcels were a nuisance. I could post letters in the box on the main road but I had to wait with the parcels until the mail van came.

Sometimes I was given braces of dead rabbits, or, worse, a still bleeding hare, to be entrusted to the driver. A mother, or a cousin, or an aunt, would be waiting at a crossroads, or at the end of a lane, by a milk churn stand somewhere.

Up in the hills most people still spoke Welsh but managed a few English words for the London girl on her borrowed black pony. They gave me cider, home-brewed, powerful stuff that it was best to be careful of if I was on the bicycle. On the more remote farms, the postman's arrival was a social event, and I learned never to be in a hurry; to be ready to stop and lean on the gate, look in on an old man or old woman indoors by the fire, speak of the weather, pass on the gossip from down the valley.

The day after the election, I drank a lot of cider. I had heard a few early results the night before but by the next morning the battery had finally died in the old wireless. 'The news will keep,' said my mother who had (inexplicably to me) voted Conservative, and was unshaken in her belief that the country 'would never turn its back on Mr Churchill'. I complained that she had corrupted my brothers by encouraging them to join a Conservative club for schoolchildren, called the Young Lions. She answered that I need not expect to find support for my traitorous opinions among the 'decent people round here'.

Although I set off (on my bike that morning) feeling frustrated, I had the most inspiring and uplifting day. A good many of the houses and farms I delivered to had electricity, either mains power or from their own generators, and almost all of them had their wirelesses on very loud indeed. As I stood on my pedals or pushed my bike uphill, or freewheeled down, the news that was so thrilling and rewarding to me boomed out from farms and cottages and barns.

'Labour gain,' the wireless said. 'Labour gain, Labour gain . . .'

It was heady stuff. I couldn't control my asinine and joyful grin, but I did manage to restrain myself from asking everyone I met which way they had voted. I guessed my mother might be right in her judgement that few of them would have voted Labour. (Or told me if they had; most farms were tenancies, belonging to one or other large local landowner, and tenants, sensibly, kept their political opinions to themselves.) But they would not have voted Conservative either. This was a Liberal constituency and the MP was Clement Davies; Clement Edward Davies, sixty-one in 1945, Liberal MP for Mongomeryshire and leader of his party; a grand old man whom no one in their senses would wish to overthrow.

I went that evening to hear him give his victory speech in Montgomery, in the market square. It was a dark and windy evening and his white hair flew around his head, but his lovely voice carried clear and effortless, without a microphone. And, remarkably it seemed to me, he was quite undaunted by the collapse of the Liberal vote elsewhere. He spoke about goodness and endeavour, about a wise and tolerant society. He was passionate in his triumph, brave, and touching. The crowd went wild and tears of joy ran down my face. It was all coming to pass. The new world, the new day, was dawning.

But when I went back to Oxford for my third and last year, the shadows were already lengthening. The war was over and Oxford was changing. The ex-servicemen were coming back, the scholars first under Class B release, seeming to us older than their actual years warranted, stern, purposeful men with wives and moustaches, taking over our university and reducing us, by their middle-aged presence, to the status of schoolchildren. There were compensations, of course: more excitement, more people – among them Tony Crosland, John Wain (who started a new small magazine called *Mandrake* and published my first short story), Henry Fairlie, John Watney, my cousin, Dr Cushing, returning to Balliol – but on the whole we felt displaced, uneasy, slightly resentful. Our streets, our cafés, our societies – the whole of our playground was invaded by demobbed soldiers and sailors and airmen; colleges where we had previously known almost everyone were full of elderly strangers; the Radcliffe Camera, so comfortably adequate for its reduced wartime population, was busy as a mainline station at rush hour.

Everything and everyone seemed so busy suddenly. The feeling that one was special, and favoured, was fading; a feeling exemplified for me by the retirement of Helen Darbishire and the appointment of Janet Vaughan as Principal of Somerville. Janet was a good appointment, a clever, worldly, efficient woman whom I respected, but I missed Helen's particular quality which was to make me feel loved and valued, not for anything I had done, or was likely to do, but for the person I was at that moment.

I wrote carefully phrased letters on Uncle Stanley's typewriter to a great many national and provincial newspapers, explaining that I really wanted to be a foreign correspondent when I left Oxford at the end of the summer but would be willing to start learning my trade at a more lowly level. I had only one answer – from the deputy editor of the *Manchester Evening News*. He asked me to go to London and meet him; I spent all the money I had on a return train ticket and a pale blue woollen jacket and borrowed a Gor-ray skirt from the girl down the corridor. My pulse raced as I walked along Fleet Street, my knees trembled. I had not given much thought to employment before. There had been no need; until the European war ended, we had all expected to be called up into one of the Armed Services when we left Oxford. The idea that I might be able to find a job on my own was new, and alarming. Why should anyone want to pay me for anything?

When I emerged from my interview I was still feeling humble and shaken, even though the nice, friendly, smiling man who offered me a job as a junior reporter had made it seem that what was a kind of miracle to me was all in the day's work to him. He had also told me that the newspaper would help me find 'respectable' digs. He said it might reassure my mother to know that.

I didn't tell her. I didn't take the job because I became engaged to one of the returning ex-servicemen, an airman who flew spotting planes for the Army; he took it for granted that we would live in London and I gave up what had been my ambition from the day Uncle Stanley gave me the typewriter without a second's thought. In fact, I was out of my depth, playing at being grown-up. My friends all said Harry Bawden, pre-war scholar of St John's, was 'so mature'; since I felt, deep down, that I was still only a frivolous schoolgirl, I should have been warned. Only two people suggested I might be making a mistake. One of Harry's aunts said I was too young, which I took as an insult, and Ken Tynan who had read my story in *Mandrake*, said that writers should never marry, they should devote their lives to art, which I thought silly.

Harry's mother came from Scotland; her family lived in Glasgow and in Edinburgh. My father was in Glasgow at the time, organising the re-fit of an armed merchant cruiser that was being returned to peacetime duty. He 'called' on Harry's aunts and uncles, which he thought was the proper thing to do, and was deeply puzzled by one uncle who said, sharply, 'You know there's money in the family, don't you? Harry will have £30,000 when his mother dies.' My impoverished father answered that he didn't call £30,000 real money; he didn't, personally, count a man as wealthy until he was a millionaire.

He was offended, all the same. He wrote from Glasgow and told me not to rush things. I was only twenty; no need to get myself tied up; what about the other young man I had been so much in love with? This letter came by the same post as one from Harry who had gone home to see his widowed mother. She had been worrying about what we would live on, apparently, and when Harry arrived he found her dead, her head in the gas oven, and all her financial documents, share certificates, bank statements, gloomy letters from the uncle who managed the family's affairs and thought I was after Harry's money, spread out on the kitchen table.

I was at home that weekend, too, staying with my mother and brothers in the house in Goodmayes which seemed to me cramped and bleak and ugly after the beauty and freedom of the country. (It must have been even more lowering for my mother who had been so happy on the farm, but I didn't think of that.) The post came while I was with the family who lived at the bottom of our garden. Their son, Ronnie, four or five years older than me, had been a rear gunner in the RAF. His plane had been shot down over France, near a small provincial town, and his parents had received a long letter from the mayor. No one in the family could read French and they had asked me to interpret for them.

Their oldest boy lived some way away; the youngest had died of a tumour on the brain. Ronnie had been their middle, and their favourite, son. They were much older than my parents. We sat at the dining-room table while the letter was fetched and smoothed out in front of me by the old man's shaking hands. They sat opposite me, frowning, silent, anxious to understand. The mayor wrote about the funeral and burial of the young Englishmen whose burned and twisted bodies had been taken from the aeroplane by the people of the town. There were details of the church service, photographs of the headstones, promises that the graves would always be cared for, and assurances of a warm welcome to anyone who came to visit the graveyard and their gallant dead. Ronnie's mother cried. His father made a fearful grimace and beat his fists upon the table. I felt this was the first time I had really understood what war could mean and was ashamed because I should not be thinking of myself, my own reaction. (Though I had loved Ronnie when I was nine or ten and he was sixteen or so. He was working in an office in the City which seemed glamorous to me, and I used to hang over the fence on Sundays, hoping to catch a glimpse of him.)

I said I would take the letter and write an English version for them and they shook their heads. I had read it to them once, they said, that was enough. They would not forget. The truth was, they didn't want to let the letter go. The father took it back from me as soon as seemed polite, folded it tenderly and put it in his inside jacket pocket, safe against his heart.

I went home to find the letter from my father and the one from Harry. I didn't show my mother my father's letter but I gave her Harry's. My mother said, 'Well, at least he's got you, poor man.'

I took my degree, and got a job with the Town and Country Planning Association, and we married in the autumn. Harry inherited the £30,000 from his mother and we bought a house in London next door to a bomb site. (In London, in the late 1940s, it was almost impossible not to buy a house next to a bomb site.) The job was dull. The Association had been run throughout the war by a middle-aged lady and a typist. After the war it had been decided to appoint a director, and the director decided that he needed an assistant. Neither he nor I could see anything to do that was not already being

Right: Edith Emily Cushing, my grandmother

Below: Aunt Bridget, Uncle Bill, Aunt Peg and Judy, my mother

Bottom left: Ellaline Ursula May, my mother, known as Judy, and 'Poll' in The Peppermint Pig

Bottom right: Charles Mabey, my father, born Mario Angelo Bennati

Teacher

Gathering flowers

At the Dancing class

*Opposite page:
some of my drawings,
age 4, as exhibited by the
Royal Drawing Society*

*Right: in 1936 wearing
a party frock made by my
grandmother*

*Left: rolling at the
farm, 1942*

*Below: my year at
Somerville – back row,
sixth from the right, with
Margaret Thatcher (neé
Roberts) to the right*

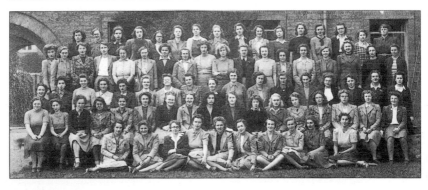

Left: a studio portrait, 1953, the year Who Calls The Tune *was published*

Below: 1976, at my desk in the house in Weybridge

Bottom: on the set of Carrie's War, *with Matthew Guiness and Rosalie Crutchley, 1976*

Niki

*Top left: Niki, Robert and
Perdita, 1959*

*Top right: my mother, Niki, Robert, me
and the dogs, early 1960s*

*Above: Robert, Terry, Cathy, Perdita,
Sue (Robert's wife) holding Sam, Niki
with Seth, our two oldest grandsons*

Right: with my dog

*Top: Austen on
the Nile*

*Above left: in Turkey, the
setting for*
George Beneath a
Paper Moon, *1972*

*Above right: in the
doorway of our Greek
house*

Right: at the taverna

With Austen, forty years on

done by the middle-aged lady and the typist, who were rightly boiling with resentment. They took it out on me by means of raised eyebrows and ostentatious sighs and affecting to be deaf when I asked a question; the director suffered less because he was a man and because he was better at pretending to be occupied. He took me out to lunch most days, as a kindly act of rescue, and fondled my knees beneath the table. He gave me a magnificent reference when I left to find another job.

Being a foreign correspondent did not seem to fit with being married. Apart from making toast or running an errand for my mother, I had never cooked or shopped before. In the country, we had lived on pheasants and partridges and wild rabbits and poacher's salmon, but there was no sign of these familiar delicacies in London shops. All that seemed to be readily available was whale meat and to make that edible required more culinary skill than I was ever likely to possess. When I was at the Town and Country Planning Association I had worked near Covent Garden and come home with bags of vegetables that I did my inefficient best with, but it seemed to take up so much time, washing them, and cutting out the bad bits. If I were working on a newspaper I might be sent off on an urgent story just as I was simmering a saucepan full of noxious green stuff on the stove. Instead, I turned my attention to magazines; writing off diligently to each one that took my fancy in the *Writers' and Artists' Yearbook*. The first that answered was a magazine about economics and politics aimed at South America. I wrote to the editor and was given an appointment with the publisher, a Mr Ernest Benn. All went swimmingly until the interview was almost at an end when he said, casually, 'By the way, you do have fluent Spanish, don't you?' He offered me another job instead but I thought (arrogantly) that the *Turkey Breeder's Gazette* was beneath my dignity.

I decided that it might be wise to look at the actual magazine before writing a flowery letter offering my services, an original approach that netted me the post of deputy editor on an industrial magazine called *Scope*. I would have worked for nothing to be called a deputy editor, but thought I ought to ask how much I would be paid. There were three men at my interview, sitting behind the table in the glossy offices of what I think must have been some new, post-war industrial association, and they all looked grave. My salary would be £900 a year, one of them said – apologetically, as if afraid I might think this inadequate.

It seemed to me riches. It was £300 more than Harry was getting as an assistant editor on the shipping magazine, *Fairplay*. I wondered earnestly if this would damage our relationship. I was also frightened; how could I possibly be worth such an enormous sum? I asked for time to think.

I went to a Lyon's tea shop and had a cup of tea; then to a news cinema in Oxford Street. I was in my seat before I realised that they were showing the film of Belsen that had recently been released. I wanted to leave, but it seemed somehow improper. Cowardice had prevented me from seeing this terrible film before, but now I was here, if only by chance, I had to see it through. If those poor people had endured it, the least I could do was sit and watch it.

I stayed until the end. I told myself I would never forget this, that I would make sure I told my children, and my children's children. And then I fainted. When I came round I was in the lobby. 'I feel sick,' I said, and was.

Someone said, 'Are you pregnant, dear?'

I shook my head indignantly, and then, in a shock of absolute surprise, realised that it was possible. I had in fact been to the contraceptive shop in Ilford; it had two entrances, one for men and one for women, which made it marginally less embarrassing, but once inside, I had been uncertain what to ask for. I muttered something about pessaries and the stern and ample lady behind the counter frowned. 'Useless,' she said, with fine contempt, and shouted over her shoulder. A small, bald man appeared, easily half her size, and together they began chanting the wares they wished to sell. I think they included a washable condom of great strength and they may have told me it would last a lifetime, but the dreadful intimacy of this encounter broke my spirit. I fled. I took no contraceptive measures. I knew I didn't want a baby, and I think I hoped that would be good enough.

'Yes,' I said, meekly, sitting up groggily on the floor of the lobby, 'I suppose I might be.'

Harry was pleased. My mother was pleased. I turned down the job of deputy editor. They said I could have eight weeks off to have the baby (an astonishingly generous offer for the late 1940s) but neither my husband nor my mother thought this was feasible. Harry said we could not afford a nanny (I hadn't dared to tell him how large my salary would be) and my mother said a baby needed its mother to take care of it or it would grow up deprived and probably become a criminal.

It was a bitter winter. The Serpentine froze over. I went sliding on the ice, and fell. I wasn't hurt, I stood up, laughing at the park keeper who was standing on the bank and watching me. But he didn't laugh back. He said, 'You shouldn't be doing that, in your condition. You ought to be ashamed of yourself. You're a grown woman, not some silly kid.'

CHAPTER FIVE

Among the Grown-Ups

The first bananas to arrive in England since before the war had reached the shops, on sale to anyone who could produce a child's ration book. The glad tidings led the BBC morning news. Niki was ten weeks old, too young for bananas, but I set out with greedy haste on my own account.

My distant, pre-war memories of bananas had been refreshed the year before: Zurich in 1947, my first visit to Europe and my first encounter with the innocence of a city that had never been at war. I bought a kilo of bananas and ate them one after the other, sitting on the parapet of a bridge and dropping the skins into the clean and shining water. A policeman stopped. 'It is forbidden in Switzerland to throw litter. There is a penalty.' I said I was sorry, though I longed to laugh: it seemed wonderfully safe to be in a country where dropping banana skins was a serious offence. The policeman said, magnanimously, 'This time I will warn you only. I see you are a foreigner and do not know our laws.'

I had bought a large and lumberly pre-war perambulator that was immensely heavy to lug up the steep flight of stairs to the front door, but light and springy on the flat. It had a sort of ledge, for shopping I suppose, but stepping on it, lightly and intermittently, made it possible to use the pram as a kind of clumsy scooter.

I scooted to the nearest greengrocer and joined the queue. Someone said it was rumoured there were onions as well as bananas but it was agreed among those of us at the end of the line that onions were too much to hope for and, in any case, they would be gone before it was our turn.

Expeditions of this kind were still a bit of a lark to me, especially if the sun was shining and the baby sleeping quietly in his springy carriage. I felt trapped indoors. But even viewed in the most optimistic spirit, the chance of buying a few onions and bananas offered only a limited diversion and the queue was very slow. I decided I had better things to do.

Exactly what, I wasn't sure. I had this baby to look after. I could push him to the park and let him lie and kick on a rug on the thin brown grass. Or I could leave the pram and take him on the bus to Marble Arch and wander round the streets of peacetime London, so unexpectedly beautiful to me that long, hot summer of 1948 that it was like discovering a new, mysterious city. I had a lot of unused energy; sometimes I carried my baby in my arms for hours, to tire myself.

I abandoned my place in the queue and left the shop. I said something like, 'Come on, young Nick, we'll skive off and paint the town.' He seemed to like it when I talked to him; he made sweet, dove-like sounds and waved his fists.

But there was no baby in the pram.

I tried to scream. Nothing much came out except a kind of breathy, mournful hooting. Enough obvious distress, however, to break up the queue. Someone sat me on a chair and forced my head down to my knees although I wasn't faint. I managed to sit up, and a glass of water was pushed against my lower lip. I gulped, and water trickled down my chin. Faces swam around me and above me; I saw each one with awful clarity, broken veins, bristly chins, each sag and pouch and wrinkle. 'She's fetching a policeman,' someone said.

Kind hands attempted to restrain me as I struggled to my feet. I looked up the road and saw the policeman, blue legs striding, a dumpy woman trotting like a little pony to keep up with him.

I gasped and fled, pushing the empty pram. Across the road, round the corner, up the street. For a frantic six or seven seconds I couldn't find my door key and began to sob with fear. Suppose, suppose . . .

But he was where I'd left him, safely lying in the middle of the bed, blowing bubbles and looking at his hands. I bent to scoop him up and cuddle him and as he saw my face he smiled; his first real baby smile, toothless and watery and cheerful and secure.

I loved him. I suppose I would have given my life for him had the need arisen. But I was alone with him all day and longed for someone to talk to who could talk back to me. Eventually, I met another girl in a similar plight. We pushed our prams to the park together on fine afternoons and, when it rained, sat in each other's houses smoking and drinking gin or whisky while our babies played behind the sofa and pulled each other's hair. Babies and boredom, boredom and babies – when the whisky ran out, we made up our faces, exchanged clothes, did our hair, and the afternoon still yawned ahead. Some evenings, we left our husbands to mind the children and went skating in Bayswater, tearing round and round the rink like young colts let out in the meadow. We met men: 'spivs' as they were called then, from whom we bought black-market butter at the corner café; medical students at the skating-rink; a rich Australian who told us that he slept with two women at once and suggested we might like to watch; a middle-aged Greek who took us to his family house in Belgravia where we danced to gramophone records in a pale, cold room with a high ceiling, while his mother and sisters looked silently on.

Even if I suffered occasionally from the disquieting feeling that I was only playing at being a wife and a mother, marking time while I waited for real life to begin, I was happy enough. Harry was an amiable husband, if sometimes low-spirited and often tired, and Niki was adaptable and easy to look after. Although much later my mother was to say that he had always been vulnerable, 'born without a shell,' she spoke with histrionic hindsight: he had been a healthy, happy baby.

After the halcyon summer of 1948, the winter came in bitter cold. The November fogs were thick as soup and a dark yellow, toasted colour; nostrils stayed black inside, lips preserved the gritty taste of soot for hours, and outdoor clothes developed a permanently clinging smell that I recognised from my mining valley days in Wales: the sulphurous smell of dusty coal. Some days it was impossible to see across the road or more than a foot ahead; strangers loomed up suddenly, banged into each other without warning. Ghosts with hacking coughs haunted alleyways. It was my first London fog and I found it romantic and exciting, but it gave Niki acute bronchitis.

Although we now had a National Health Service doctor, an excellent man who had once captained England for rugger, the doctor who had delivered Niki and looked after him the first months of his life was a paediatrician who had written a book about babies which contained some unexceptionable advice and one singularly dotty idea. Babies, the theory ran, were well- insulated creatures, capable of preserving their own body warmth; to swaddle them in too many clothes damaged their natural thermostat as well as inhibiting their muscle development by preventing them from kicking freely. They should spend as much time as possible lying naked in the open air, even in cold weather. Flat-dwellers, all those without access to a convenient open space, were advised to construct a cage and hang the baby out of the window.

I wasn't that daft. But perhaps Niki wore fewer clothes than was sensible. The paediatrician's good book had said that as long as a child's chest was warm, cold hands and feet did not matter. 'A warm chest means he's alive and that's all,' my mother said, rubbing ointment on his chilblains.

He coughed and coughed. In the spring, our rugger-playing NHS doctor said we should take him out of London before the next winter. I got on a Green Line bus, took a ticket to the end of the line, to Chertsey, in Surrey, went to the first estate agent I came across and found a solid Georgian house with a good garden. We moved a month later.

When Niki was three I had another son, Robert, and two years later left their father for another man. I met Austen on a bus; he was married, with two daughters, an ex-naval officer who was now a journalist. Our divorces went through expeditiously with the usual wailing and complaint and self-justification for bad behaviour on our part. Austen's daughters went to South Africa with their mother; my sons stayed with us. Austen and I were still in our twenties when we married and the boys were young enough to accept him as a father. For Robert, Daddy was a synonym for Austen. When Niki was nine, and Robert six years old, we had a daughter, Perdita.

Niki was at boarding-school then, at a school his father had chosen for him, but Austen and I had not been unwilling to send him. He was a clever child who had been bored at the local school, or so we told ourselves. And, on my part, I was affected by a kind of anxious snobbery. Both my husbands and most of our friends had been to boarding preparatory schools and public schools and assumed that their children, especially their sons, would do the same. State educated myself, I secretly thought private education both a waste of money and socially poisonous, but lacked the courage, or perhaps the conviction, to say so. I merely determined that if Niki was unhappy, we would bring him home.

But he appeared to enjoy the school in Kent. My parents lived a bus ride away and my mother often went to take him out on Sundays. She said, much later, that he always clung to her hand when it was time for her to leave, and begged her to catch a later bus. I said it was an act, put on for Granny, which was partly true. Niki had always cultivated pathos when it suited him, but I was also comforting myself. I hated taking him back to school after a weekend, leaving him to stand alone at the school gate, gazing wistfully after our departing car, abandoned and forlorn.

He was a loving, valiant child. Once, when he overheard us groaning about some alarming and unexpected bill, he packed up his best toys, weeping, and gave them to us to sell. And one summer holiday, when he jumped off a breakwater and landed on a nail and the matron at the cottage hospital stitched up his foot without an anaesthetic, he sat quite still on Austen's lap and made no sound. But my mother had been right when she had called him vulnerable. He was more fragile than his brother and sister, more unsure of himself, more easily upset, and as he grew older, in his teens, his fragility became more apparent. Sometimes you could see his face betraying inner terror, as if he were shivering inside his skin.

He went to Westminster as a day boy. To begin with all seemed well;

he enjoyed the freedom, and the work. He rowed until his bad circulation was diagnosed as Raynaud's Disease and, at about the same time, he began to do less well in class. He picked fights with his younger brother, hurting him quite savagely sometimes, purging his jealousy. And there were other things. He was hard to wake in the morning. Well, that was natural at his age and the daily journey to London was tiring. But he had grown slovenly and inert; he didn't always undress at night and when he finally appeared at the breakfast table it was often in the crumpled clothes that he had slept in. Persuading him to take a bath required tenacity and cunning; getting him to have his hair cut was beyond all diplomacy. He would smile and do nothing.

The length of a young man's hair was a curious obsession of the early 1960s; it split not only generations but families apart, divided them as nothing else had done since the Suez crisis of 1956. Grandparents made a particular moral issue out of it and sometimes blamed the boy's parents, their children, for not 'taking a stand' against a young man's flowing locks. We knew of one grandfather who had actually crept into a grandson's bedroom one night and cut off all the hair from one side of his head while he was sleeping. Parents who had a teenage boy tried not to meet *their* parents on a family occasion unless they had to. Christmases were ruined; women wept, men ordered each other out of the house.

To those of us who belonged to the trapped middle generation, between elderly, complaining parents and indignant adolescents, the hair hysteria seemed to last for ever. In fact, by the time Robert was old enough to grow a beard, his pretty, curly, shoulder-length hair elicited no more reproof from, say, my father, than a chuckling, frequently repeated, little joke 'J.C., that's who you remind me of! J.C.' Niki's hair was never as long as Robert's (nor so clean and tended, either) but he suffered more.

He was sent home from school one day, forbidden to return until his hair was cut. He took his guitar and climbed through the window of his bedroom and sat outside, on the steep, slippery roof, playing the guitar and singing in a growling monotone. Grey rain fell upon him steadily. He refused to come in until Austen came home –

summoned out of a meeting in mid morning. While he coaxed our son indoors and took him to a barber, I telephoned the school. I was prepared to be furious, but Niki's housemaster silenced me. Of course, on the surface, it must seem unreasonable, a fuss about nothing, but in Niki's case, this good man said, he thought the long and dirty hair was not just ordinary rebellion and resentment but something deeper. He thought we should think about professional help. In fact – he hated to say this, and I believed he really *did* hate it – the school was not prepared to have him back unless he saw a psychiatrist.

A mild depression was not uncommon in adolescents, we were told. It would probably pass by itself but it might be sensible to hurry up the process with some pills. They wouldn't cure him, he was immature and had certain personality problems that only time would set right. But pills would help. Perk him up. Get him through this sticky patch.

The psychiatrist was a thin-faced, solemn man behind a desk. He had already seen Niki – who had smartened himself up to go to the hospital; put on a clean shirt, polished his shoes.

Austen asked, why was he immature? Anxiety made him angry, adversarial. He sounded as if he were challenging the psychiatrist to a duel. The man said, gently, that the clinical answer would be that at some point or other Niki had failed to make the right transference. No doubt, if we kept at it we might come up with something but it would only be guesswork, no practical help. He smiled and said, 'If you want theories, Mr Kark, ask your wife, she's the novelist.'

That made me feel stupid. As if he were laughing at me. Embarrassed, I said I didn't know what he meant about personality problems. If he had asked me a year ago what Niki was like, I would have said a normal lively boy. More emotional than some, perhaps more sensitive than most. Now, I didn't know. He had changed, but not in any positive way. I stopped before I said he was jealous of his brother, even though he loved him. I didn't want to appear to complain about Niki to this stranger: on the contrary, I wanted to defend him.

But he nodded, as if I had, without meaning to, told him what he wanted to know. He said he had found Niki a gentle and delightful boy. He didn't think there was any grave problem. The drinking would stop once he was less depressed and it was a great thing to be thankful for that he was not abusing drugs. He thought perhaps a few months' therapy might help but a therapist must be chosen very carefully. Niki was clever, quite manipulative; he needed someone not only intelligent but *quick*.

And near to his own age. The psychiatrist smiled; a practised, deprecating smile. 'I am too old,' he said. 'He could run rings around me.'

And Niki had run rings around him, we found out later. But for the moment we were no more than bewildered. Niki drank a glass of wine at meals sometimes, but he was rarely out late, and never, to our knowledge, came home drunk. And how would we not know?

We thought we were watchful parents. Watchful, but not oppressive. And we were in that heady period of life when you are absolutely certain you can keep your children safe from harm by taking thought and timely action. We were bringing up three handsome, happy, clever children. One had had a little setback but a few pills, the right therapist, would soon put him right. We knew very little about illegal drugs; there had been none around when we were young, and our children were still too young to have been exposed to them.

Or so we thought. It wasn't wilful blindness, simply ignorance. This was the beginning of the 1960s. We were a middle-class family in suburban England. In the Surrey town we lived in now, in a big, old, Edwardian villa near a mainline station, they still played cricket on the green on summer evenings and the grocer, the fishmonger, the greengrocer and the butcher still delivered anything you wanted at a moment's notice. Our back door was only locked at night; in daytime it was always open for the convenience of tradesmen, plumbers, children; we knew no one who had installed a burglar alarm.

All the same we went to see John Carleton, the Head Master of Westminster. We had not been impressed with him before, he was so smooth, so bland and polished, but he was affable enough on this occasion. We asked about drugs and he said drugs were absolutely not a problem at the school. We told each other that the speed with which he made this disclaimer was not necessarily suspicious: other parents, older and more worldly-wise than we were must have asked this question long before we thought of it. And he sounded so confident and certain.

Niki said the therapist was a waste of his time and our money. He looked a little sly, as if he wasn't sure I would believe this. Perhaps she had been harder to hoodwink than the psychiatrist at the hospital? He said that he had work to do if he was going to pass his A levels and get into university; that's what we *wanted*, wasn't it? Well, of course it was. But it was what he wanted, too.

He didn't do as well as he had hoped, and his teachers had expected, but well enough to get a place at Kent University to read Classics. He seemed to have a happy first year, making friends and writing poetry. Just before the summer vacation he said he wanted to go to America with a group of friends, but didn't seem unduly upset when we said we hadn't got the money, why hadn't he asked us earlier, given us more time? He took a job instead, in Whitbread's brewery, and lodged in Maida Vale with a BBC producer – to us, any association with the BBC ensured respectability.

We were worried, all the same; a distant, nagging ache. We met him in a pub in Warwick Avenue, a pub I knew from the time I lived in Maida Vale. We used to call it the Polish pub because it was haunted by Polish ex-servicemen – *haunted* was an apt word: I had thought them rather frightening men, cold-eyed, remote.

I told Niki this. I asked him if he remembered being pushed round these streets as a baby. Prattling on, fuelled by anxiety, I thought his eyes glazed with boredom. Suddenly he launched into speech. There was a girl where he was living, another lodger, who was on drugs, taking huge quantities of LSD. He, Niki, had warned her it could blow her mind. He proceeded to lecture us on the dangers of drugs with such force and cogency that we began to feel guilty. How could we have suspected him for a moment, this decent young man, so aware of the hazards, so concerned for others.

He went back to Kent at the end of the summer. Halfway through the term we had a telephone call from his college. Niki was in the sick-bay. He appeared to be suffering from some kind of schizoid breakdown: he was numb, shut away, incapable of making any response beyond the politely social. (He was always polite – heart-breakingly so when he was very ill: it led some of our more insensitive friends to remark, challengingly, as if we had an interest in his continuing illness, that he seemed perfectly *normal* to them.)

I drove to Kent to pick him up. He was gentle and passive and unusually, if superficially, clean; one of his girlfriends had washed his hair. On the way home, he said, 'I've had a lot of LSD, Mum. I think it's damaged my brain.'

The gullible psychiatrist he had seen originally was obviously out of the question. We wanted someone we could trust and, to our relief, Peter Dally, the chief consultant at the Westminster Hospital, a good friend who had known Niki since he was a small boy, offered to take care of him. Niki was admitted to Peter's hospital where he sat in bed surrounded by books he could no longer read but liked to have by him – for protection? for magic? – smiling engagingly at the other patients, at the pretty nurses, at all his visitors. But that was all. He wasn't functioning – functioning was the word the doctors used for the activities that distinguish human beings from cabbages; from making decisions to finishing sentences, and keeping themselves clean. In common with many mental patients he had body lice. The sister expected us to be shocked; she took us into her office to tell us the grim news in such hushed, grave tones that although it seemed to us a minor matter in our poor son's dreadful circumstances, we did not dare to say so.

They gave him pills at first, and when the pills didn't work, ECT and insulin. He was lucky; this was an acute unit in a good hospital and he had a brilliant doctor. He was taught how to make wicker baskets and I am ashamed to remember that I thought this kind of therapy 'beneath him'. I took him a beautifully bound notebook with thick, creamy pages and suggested he wrote down things that struck him about this whole experience. It was not one he might have chosen, perhaps, but that was no reason for not making full use of it, turning it into something positive instead of negative! It was an opportunity in a way! Grist to the mill for anyone who wanted to *write*, for example! All these other patients in the ward, all different, from different backgrounds, but all at some crisis in their lives so it would be easier to see beneath the surface!

Niki smiled at me crookedly, looking suddenly like a tired, old man. He said, 'I'm not likely to be a writer, Mum. And they're all roaring nuts. I don't see what's so interesting about roaring nuts.'

'Oh, come,' I said. I heard myself laugh as if firing a gun. 'What about that nice boy with a beard, the one you were playing chess with last night? What makes him tick?'

'Heroin makes him tick,' Niki said.

He had not, it appeared, used heroin himself. We found syringes in a drawer in his room, and some white powder. Peter sent it off for analysis, but it was only baking powder. There was some comfort in this, we were told: the hallucinogenic drugs, pot and LSD, though damaging, were not addictive. (I cannot remember who told us this: we sought information from anyone and everyone, hungry for the smallest crumb of comfort.)

He came slowly back to life. A sort of life. He was home for Christmas; gentle, withdrawn and biddable. We played the old party game of making lists of rivers, countries, famous people, all beginning with a letter chosen at random. This was a game we often played on family occasions, having found that children with good memories and nimble minds could defeat the grown-ups. We had not meant to play this year for fear that Niki would feel humiliated if he couldn't make a reasonable showing, but it was Niki who suggested we should play. He won, quite easily, and Austen had to leave the room to blow his nose and dry his tears in private. Absurd, of course, to feel such disproportionate relief but we clutched at each and every straw.

After Christmas, Austen's older daughter, Cathy, came to visit from South Africa. She had not seen the boys for many years but as soon as she walked through the front door it was as if she had always lived with us. She and Robert made toffee, laughing in the kitchen; tobogganing on St Ann's Hill in Chertsey, she dragged Niki up the icy slopes like a loving, bossy sister, until he began to look rosy and properly alive. A healthy young man with a future.

I took him to Tunisia, on holiday. He bought a voluminous, hooded, black burnous that enveloped him completely, and wore it most of the time, his face shrouded from view. I hired a car and drove into the desert to look at Roman ruins. We stopped in an oasis town and the little children crowded round him, looking, I assumed, for money or sweets, but he gave them nothing, just stood still, and after a while they began to move close to him, to touch him. They were pretty children, little and thin, with great, dark, sad eyes. I left him to wander round the town and on the way back, saw him coming towards me through a white archway, the children fluttering behind and around him, clinging to his hands, his clothes. I wondered later if he had bought hashish from them but at the time I only thought, senti-mentally, that he looked like the Pied Piper.

Nothing that happened to him happened in isolation, of course. We had spent most evenings at the hospital and Robert was left at home to persuade his eleven-year-old sister to have supper and go to bed. Perdita could not understand what was wrong with Niki. (We hardly understood ourselves; how could we explain to her?) She knew people went into hospital to have operations and she decided that Niki must have appendicitis with complications and that was why we didn't take her to see him. She didn't tell us this until much later. My mother and father, equally bewildered, came to the con-clusion that Niki's illness was some kind of wicked wilfulness; at the very least, a deplorable weakness in his character. They didn't say so directly, or not to us, anyway, but the implication was there in my mother's lack of response when we spoke on the telephone; in her silences and martyred sighs, in the questions that were meaningfully limited to the health of the other two children. Austen's parents were more restrained but this made me angry because I took restraint for indifference: Niki was not their grandson, no blood rela-tion, so why should they care?

It made us so angry! More than angry – a roaring rage filled us both when we contemplated our four parents and their lack of understanding and support. Indeed, although we were fortunate in our friends who were not only sympathetic but immensely forbearing, listening to us interminably, practical support was hard to find. Peter thought it might help Niki to live in some kind of therapeutic community for a while; a halfway house between hospital and home. The Westminster's welfare department tried to find him a hostel, and failed. Apparently all suitable hostels had such long waiting lists that Niki's name would have had to be put down at birth to find a place in one. I wrote to a place in Richmond, run by charity, to which I had once sent a small donation after reading a glowing description of its achievements in a magazine in our dentist's waiting room, but when they finally replied (after several weeks, a longer period than I would have expected from the caring image they projected) they said Niki was too young for them, too ill. I wrote to a monastery which we had heard sometimes cared for men who had had some kind of crisis in their lives, treating them as lay brothers and providing an undemanding atmosphere of peace, quiet, and healthy living. We had great hopes of this place until they wrote back and said they had given up their work with their 'handicapped brethren' in order to concentrate on their retreats for businessmen.

A muscular Christian who ran a farm-based community in Dorset was more welcoming. We took Niki there – still wearing his black burnous. He seemed happy to stay and we were moderately happy to leave him. We told ourselves that even if we found the morally uplifting atmosphere oppressive, he might find it restful. And the surroundings were beautiful.

He had been there a week when they rang from a local hospital to say he had been brought in unconscious. The muscular Christian, disapproving of drugs of any kind, had decided that Niki should not be taking the medication the hospital had given him. He had confiscated his pills, prayed with him, lectured him on the importance of fresh air and exercise and sent him out to work on the farm.

We brought our son home. It seemed safer. Peter Dally agreed. (We were lucky in Peter: he did not hold to the fashionable view that families, especially mothers, were to blame when their children fell ill.) And in fact, Niki seemed better; well enough, anyway, to make a disastrous decision for himself. He wanted to go back to Kent in the autumn term.

*

He did no work. He failed his exams. He rang us from Canterbury late one night, angry and weeping. It was a plot by the faculty. Oh, they had persuaded *us* they were civilised and reasonable but that was just a mark of their cunning. They had marked him down from the beginning. Victimisation was the name of their game! He had spoken to lawyers, who had urged him to take the matter up in the courts. It would be a test case.

We talked to him, in turn, for hours. Afterwards, we said to each other that he must be drunk. Or drugged. Either was preferable to what we had both separately thought, which was that he had sounded mad.

And yet, when he came home, he was our sweet son; reasonable, well-mannered, logical. He had failed his exams because his motorbike had broken down. He was sharing a cottage in Whitstable with a friend and there was no suitable bus to take him to Canterbury. We did not ask how the friend managed to attend his lectures and seminars. We blamed his tutor instead. At *Oxford*, so we told each other, if a student had failed to turn up for tutorials, his tutor would have gone to look for him. At least made enquiries! It was disgraceful, the lack of pastoral care in these new universities! We discovered that indignation was a fine defence against despair.

From then on, there were good times and bad times, and times that were neither good nor bad, only confusing. His girlfriend had a baby, Niki's daughter, and they married, found a small flat in Kilburn, and were happy for a while. He did his best to find and keep jobs; in a City bank, in the Civil Service, in the gramophone library of the BBC. He could always make a good first impression but he couldn't keep it up, hold himself together. It was as if he was splintered inside, like a parcel of broken glass.

He refused to see a doctor. His wife left him. He stayed alone in their flat for a while and then came to live with us again. He had decided – this was his idea, not ours – that he would go to the Law College at Guildford, which was conveniently close. By this time, Robert was a medical student at Guy's Hospital and living in London, and Perdita was in Glasgow, working at a garage, on the pumps, and later as a milkman, while she waited for a job in the Citizens' Theatre.

Living with us, a solitary child in his mid-twenties, Niki did not seem outwardly unhappy. He walked the dog. He and Austen played chess together. He had favourite television programmes, sentimental old films late at night, *Doctor Who* on Saturdays, that he liked us to watch with him. I reminded him to clean his teeth. Austen straightened his shirt collar and his tie for him most mornings. In the evenings he would talk about his day at the Law College. The things he said were interesting and intelligent, concealing from us, and possibly from himself, that the work was beyond him because he could not write it down. This boy, who had written poetry, who had always been exact with words, was unable to complete a sentence on paper. *Word-blocked* is the technical term, and when we heard it we recognised the truth of it: Niki could write a word, or sometimes two, and then it was as if a shutter had come down in his mind; a guillotine upon his hand.

He took the dog for a walk one winter night. He came back, soaked to the skin, shivering, laughing. He said, 'I thought it would be easy to drown, but the river was too cold, and the dog kept barking on the bank.'

We ran a hot bath for him. We gave him a whisky toddy. We put his wet clothes in the washing machine. We put him to bed and sat with him while he told us about the pains that were paralysing his arm so that he couldn't write, about the damage some Nigerians – what Nigerians? – had done to him that was numbing his brain. We stayed awake all night, visiting his room every half an hour or so. He slept soundly, barely moving. At breakfast, we persuaded him to stay at home until Hugh, our GP and friend, had been to see him. Niki made no objection; indeed, he agreed to everything we said to him. He was admitted to the local psychiatric hospital, an enormous towered and turreted asylum with stained-glass windows and gardens full of rhododendrons. He was put into a ward that was locked 'because some of our guests might want to leave us', the male sister told us archly.

He was there the rest of that winter. Perhaps because he was so exceptionally untidy, he was given a pleasant, small room to himself off the main dormitory. He had a good many visitors and there was no check on the presents that they took him. A good deal of the time he seemed lethargic and sleepy, but when we spoke to the staff about this they said we were not to worry, he wasn't taking anything he shouldn't, only the medication he was being given. Although it was an easygoing place, comfortable and friendly, it was difficult to find anyone to talk to who could – or would – tell us anything about our son's condition. It was borne in on us, slowly, that the staff, the nursing staff at any rate, saw us as interfering parents and Niki as a grown man who must be protected from our intrusive curiosity. One of the nurses said, 'You must ask him yourself. He will tell you what he wants you to know.'

And yet, when he ran away, they expected us to bring him back as if he were an errant child. We returned him once, with the help of his brother, and left him weeping in his locked ward and raging about the Nigerians. The second time, we refused. He had rung us to say where he was, in his flat in London, and we asked him what he wanted to do. He said he would stay there for a couple of nights to 'sort a few things out', and then come home to us.

But that evening, he was picked up by the police for possession of cannabis resin. They had burst into the flat, waving a warrant and yelling abuse, and refusing to believe that he had just arrived, straight from hospital. They searched the flat and found the cannabis and a small amount of heroin – which may or may not have belonged to him: various friends had occupied the flat in the six months he had been living out of London.

He telephoned us from Brixton Prison and asked for some clean clothes so that he could look respectable in the magistrates' court the next morning. Although we broke speed limits driving up from Surrey, we arrived too late. The enormous sergeant behind a grille yelled at us as if we were delinquents on a parade ground. Clean clothes had to be produced before 5.30. Austen shouted back and thumped the counter. Our son was *on remand*, not a convicted villain. There was a murmur of approval from the crowded waiting room, loud enough to encourage the officer to think again. He muttered that we would have to wait for a receipt, took the clothes, and closed the grille.

I was a magistrate. I had sent people to prison. This was my first experience of life on the other side. We sat on narrow benches; the atmosphere was lively, our neighbours friendly in an open, cheerful way. Most of them carried the smart plastic bags supplied by Harrods Food Hall. 'It's different, them being on remand like,' someone explained when I asked what one was allowed to bring.

Until the receipt arrived and our name was called, we chatted socially with the other waiting visitors, a tiny bit *de haut en bas* perhaps, a minute element of condescension on our part, but then we were so sure that we were only here by some ridiculous mischance, that the proper order of things would shortly be restored and we would be seen for the worthy bourgeois folk we were. Tomorrow, Niki would make a brief appearance in court and be remanded to a later date. Eventually he would be fined perhaps, even put on probation on condition he went back to hospital, but in the meantime he would be free.

When he was remanded in custody, we were incredulous. We re-assured each other – it was a mistake, a ludicrous miscarriage of justice – but we had passed, without knowing it, through a barrier. On the other side the rules of the game were not ones we knew.

At first, we didn't understand this. Once we had rung our lawyer and taken advice, the system appeared to work in our favour. It cost £100 to get bail for Niki from a Judge in Chambers; a lot to us at that time, but manageable. We went to the Law Courts, that lovely, pre-posterous, fairytale castle in the City of London, and scuttled up and down the warren of halls and turrets and twisting stairways behind an usher in a black gown until we found where 'our' judge was sitting. Once we had tracked him down, our application for bail was allowed in a matter of minutes. We had to take the Order of Release to a police station to get an official form to present at the prison, but that was just a formality, our lawyer said comfortingly. He shook hands and left us. Austen looked at his watch. He had a meeting. But he had time to go with me to Bow Street police station.

The reception area was painted acid green. There was an old woman muttering on a bench by the wall and a young policeman behind the counter. He glanced at the Order and shook his head. He couldn't deal with this, we had to sign 'the book' and he had no authority. The duty officer would be back from lunch at about two o'clock.

It wasn't yet midday. I said something about a long lunch hour. Austen said we had been told this was just a formality. The young policeman shrugged his shoulders, then told us, grudgingly, that the book was locked up. The bail register. The duty officer had the key. We could wait if we liked. Or go away and come back.

We waited. We sat on the bench beside the old woman. She was wearing a fur coat – fur from an animal that must have died some time in the last century – and pink slippers on her little, veined, bare feet. She whispered to me, 'They don't care, do they? The hours you spend waiting.'

Austen lost his temper in the end, so effectively that a senior police-man was summoned in a matter of minutes, apologies offered and the business concluded. Austen went to his meeting and I took a taxi to Brixton Prison feeling vaguely ashamed because we had used our loud and educated voices to get what we wanted and left the old lady in pink slippers still waiting, ignored, unattended. Privilege, however, ended at the prison gate. 'Magistrate?' the officer asked. 'No,' I said, 'prisoner's Mum', and he stopped smiling. I barely had time to pass the form to him before he slammed the door on my fingers.

I waited for Niki in a hut outside the gate, a kind of Portakabin, run by some kind of prisoners' aid association and staffed by volun-teers. It was warm inside the hut; I was given a cup of tea and a biscuit by a gentle, middle-aged woman in a flowered apron. We talked a lit-tle, I can't now remember what about, only that she soothed and calmed me like the best of mothers, and that when Niki arrived she gave him a cup of tea and made him laugh.

He was pleased to be home. All the same, he said, time served on remand would come off an eventual sentence, so it might have been better to leave him where he was. The weeks before the court hearing he seemed to be deliberately preparing himself for martyrdom; when we pointed out that since he was a first offender there would have to be social and psychiatric reports before he could be sent to prison, he kept quiet, as if pitying our innocence. In Willesden magistrates' court, when he was given a sentence of six months, he turned round briefly, searching for us in the public gallery, and when he found us, smiled wryly, and held his hands out, palms upward, shrugging.

As we came down the stairs from the public gallery, the policeman from the drug squad, who had prepared the prosecution papers for Niki's case, was waiting for us. He said, 'I'm sorry about this. It should never have happened.'

Niki had been unlucky – in the court, the bench, and in the clerk, who had retired with the magistrates instead of waiting to be called when they had made their decision, as is the proper course. (Later, when we complained to the Lord Chancellor's Office we were told that the clerk would be disciplined.) The magistrates had not asked for social and psychiatric reports as they should have done on a first offender with a history of mental illness. When I questioned Niki's barrister he said that asking for reports on first offenders was only a Home Office directive, without the force of law, and in busy inner city courts like Willesden, this was often disregarded. He admitted that the sentence would probably be overturned on appeal, but Niki had already told him that he had made up his mind to stick it out in prison, and 'get it over with'.

I went to see him in the cellars below the court. The tiled walls ran with water and there was a smell of sweat and seaweed. The cells were the size of small lavatories and there seemed to be two men in each. Niki's companion was a muscular man with oddly short, bare, freckled arms, wearing shrunken jeans and a pale blue T-shirt. He had a pleasant face and clear grey eyes. He didn't look like a criminal. But neither did Niki, who was wearing the half-glasses he sometimes affected and reading Henri Troyat's *Life of Tolstoy* in the Penguin edition. At least, he was pretending to read it. I tried to persuade him to appeal and he said it wasn't worth the trouble, it wasn't as if he had a job to go to and at least he wouldn't have to go back to that hospital. He said, 'I don't want a report that says I'm mad. There's nothing wrong with my mind. What's wrong with me is physical.'

He was taken to Wormwood Scrubs. One of the other two men in his cell was also a first offender, a man who had killed his wife when he found her in bed with the landlord. He and Niki played chess together and the murderer usually won. The first time we went to the prison, Niki said that his new friend complained that he lacked the competitive spirit.

At one end of the visitors' room, a warder sat behind a raised desk. There was a table for each prisoner and his one or two visitors, and a counter where another warder sold coffee and biscuits. The effect was that of a schoolroom temporarily turned into a café; a coffee morning conducted for some educational purpose under the teacher's eye. Our conversation with Niki was jovial. He looked well if a little pale, and very clean. He answered our questions politely, but was happier asking questions himself: how were Robert and Perdita? When was Robert getting married? He was sorry he couldn't come to the wedding. How was Margaret, *Marge*, the nice woman who had helped us take care of our household and children since Niki was three years old? How were Granny and Grandad? Would we give them all his love?

He looked doubtful, a little shy; so did we, I imagine. We were all three uncertain how to behave in this situation. Feeling that he was the host perhaps put an extra burden on him. He tried to make us laugh. The third man in his cell was an ex-Borstal boy who was so tidy, Niki said, that he and the wife-murderer were much discomfited. Of course, it was the way the Borstal boy had been trained, but it was hard on his cell mates who hadn't had his advantages.

We laughed over-heartily. A prison officer with ruddy cheeks and a curling moustache that made him look like a Victorian villain appeared at the end of the room with a handbell. He clanged it briefly, with some thoughtful delicacy, and we all rose like school-children at the end of a lesson. Niki leaned across the table to kiss us goodbye. He said, 'Thank you for coming.'

The next week, a psychiatrist in the prison service telephoned us. He had visited the Scrubs and admitted Niki to the prison hospital. He was schizophrenic and suicidal and, in his opinion, and in the opinion of several other doctors who had examined him, should be transferred directly from Wormwood Scrubs to a secure ward in the Westminster as soon as he had served his sentence.

*

He went back to Peter's care, to our relief. If he felt bitter about not being set free, merely moved from one prison to another, he didn't show it. In fact, he seemed surprisingly content, flirting with the nurses, playing chess (this time with a headwaiter from a famous London restaurant who was in a clinical depression), and making a cushion. At least, that is what he said he was making. We never saw it.

After a few weeks, he was allowed to leave the hospital for part of the day. We used to meet him at the War Museum at the back of Westminster Hospital; sometimes we took sandwiches and sat in the garden. He was pleased to see us. He was no longer thought to be suicidal, and the worst of his schizophrenic symptoms, the demons that plagued him, seemed to be controlled by drugs. We didn't discuss his illness; if we tried to, he became agitated and repeated what he had said to me in the dungeons under Willesden magistrates' court, that there was nothing wrong with his mind, what ailed him was physical. Since a chemical imbalance is thought to be one of the causes of schizophrenia, this did not seem an unreasonable statement, and we did not repeat it to Peter. We wanted to do what was best for Niki. But we also wanted to be on his side; to agree with him, placate him, and this sometimes made us edit what we told his doctors.

We had just sold our ugly but comfortable house in Weybridge and bought a much smaller, terraced house in Islington, suitable for a middle-aged couple whose children had left them. Robert had married in the spring; Perdita was still in Glasgow; my sweet stepdaughter, Teresa, who had been living with us, had found a flat in London; the social workers in the welfare department of Westminster Hospital were confident they would find a suitable place for Niki to live when he was discharged. They told us that schizophrenics should never live with their families, least of all with their parents; the stress was intolerable for the calm management of a delicate mind that should be sheltered from emotion, from the claustrophobic demands and expectations of family life.

We trusted them. We believed that a trained social worker must know better than we could possibly do. Two days before we moved house, the telephone rang. Niki said, 'They're letting me out, Mum. I'll be home this evening.'

I said, 'How wonderful, darling.' As soon as I had put the receiver down, I rang the welfare department. There must be some mistake. Oh, no, the social worker said, there was no mistake: it had just proved quite impossible to find a place for Niki. He didn't seem to fit in anywhere. He was clearly unsuitable for a mentally handicapped home and he wasn't physically disabled. She made it sound as if this was somehow Niki's fault; that he should have made more effort to get the right qualifications.

I pointed out to the crisp, dismissive voice at the other end of the telephone that we had been told that we were bad for him, that the worst thing that could happen to someone like Niki was having to live with his parents.

'That's quite true,' the crisp voice said. 'But there is no one else who will take him, is there?'

I like to think I thanked the voice for being so encouraging, but that may only be *esprit de l'escalier*, from which I often suffer.

We might be bad for him, but we were overjoyed to have him home and free. Moving to London was an excellent diversion, providing him with practical things to do that were of obvious assistance to us all. Austen bought new hi-fi equipment and he and Niki went to Islington early in the morning of the day we moved, to install it in the new house, and to spare him what I thought might be the distress of watching the removal from the old. In fact, I suppose I was thinking of myself; the distress at leaving home was mostly mine.

We had lived in this house in Weybridge for thirteen years and our children had grown up there. Sweeping up after the men had gone off with the furniture, sitting on the stairs with our elderly mongrel bitch and waiting for the taxi that was to take me to London, I found myself suddenly nostalgic for happy times that were no more. On the journey to London, I sat with the old dog on my lap and wept against her silky neck. Arriving, I managed a bright face, but later on, quite late that evening, after we had dined in Camden Passage, I found myself bawling in the street, uncontrollably, mouth open, tears streaming. Austen and Niki put their arms around me. Niki said, 'It's being uprooted, Mum. Mandrakes scream when they're pulled up, why shouldn't you?'

While we were busy, rearranging furniture, unpacking books, fixing the electrics, exploring the neighbourhood and shopping – while we were all three doing these practical things together, he knew he was useful. But when Austen went back to the BBC and I went back to my typewriter, finding him dignified occupation became more difficult. He spent a long time reading the newspapers in the morning and doing the crossword. He took the dog for long walks. He and I went to the cinema in the late afternoons.

He met a girl; a Swedish au pair, kind and pretty. He became slowly more sociable, took her out on his motorbike, and walking on Hampstead Heath. He was proud to be living normally again, to have found a girl. We didn't tell her he had been mentally ill. We had told very few people since we moved to London, and only our close friends knew that he had been to prison. We had grown used to secrecy over the months, partly for Niki's sake, because it was what he wanted, but also to spare my mother. At the time Niki had been arrested my father was dying and it seemed the wrong moment to break the kind of news she would find shocking as well as distressing. Now, she had moved to London to live near to me and my brother, and would be mortified to find out her grandson had a criminal record that might be known to her neighbours. But we should have told the nice Swedish girl.

Eventually he told her himself in his own way. He told her that he was dying from a crippling illness that affected his bones and his bowels. His body was rotting while he was still alive. He had been beaten up by Nigerians. He dare not go to a doctor because doctors were evil and dangerous. They had ruined his life. He was a poet but they had put him in a straitjacket of medication and he could no longer write poetry. He drank too much. One night he crushed a glass in his hand.

She came to us then, and we told her the truth. Or the truth as we knew it. She tried to persuade him to see the psychiatrist at the Whittington Hospital, which was where the Westminster had sent him to continue his therapy, and broke off the friendship when he refused to go. We went instead, hoping for guidance, as we went to lectures at Morley College that had been arranged by the National

Schizophrenia Association. The psychiatrist encouraged and advised us, and the lectures were illuminating. And perhaps, helping us, they helped Niki a little, by proxy.

His social worker, on the other hand, helped him not at all. She was a big, blonde young woman with protuberant blue eyes like pale jelly. Her chief concern was to remind us at regular intervals that we must 'expect nothing' from Niki. 'Your son,' she said consolingly, 'is nothing but a shell.'

Niki fled when she came to the house. She sat in our living room telling us how fortunate we were that Niki could cross the road to buy his own cigarettes. Daring to answer back at last, we said that had never been Niki's problem and asked her when she had last talked to him. She said, not for several months: the social workers at the Whittington were taking industrial action, refusing to deal directly with patients. When she had gone Niki crept cautiously out of his room. He said, 'You must be mad to let her in.'

Austen had an operation on his feet. The day he came home, Niki woke up in a new girlfriend's bed with German measles. She kept him with her, looked after him, found him a gardening job. She was young, intelligent, good-natured, and he settled in with her; they lived together round the corner. He was working hard, getting up sometimes at five in the morning to go to the flower market. But he was happy with his girl, with his motorbike. He passed his test to drive a motor car and bought an old van. Then he began to say that his pains were crippling him. They were so bad now that he could no longer manage even the lightest manual work; he would have to look for an office job. He applied for a course in computer programming, taking an aptitude test on which he scored highly. We were afraid for him but it seemed wrong to discourage him. We said, at least have a holiday first. We took him to a friend's house in the Auvergne, and he enjoyed himself, reading maps, planning expeditions, scything the grass in the summer meadow.

He came home brown and well. But he couldn't complete the computer course. Another car went into his van at a crossroads and it wasn't worth mending. His girlfriend fell in love with someone else and threw him out. He turned up one evening, tears spurting.

We did our best to comfort him but found it an effort. Unsurprisingly, perhaps, we were at odds with each other and it made us feel tired and useless: if we were unhappy together, how could we expect to help Niki? Moving back into the house, he sensed our despair and tried to console us, making me cups of tea, pouring drinks and cooking supper when Austen came home in the evening. He refused to go back to see Peter, perhaps fearing Peter's acuity, but he agreed to go to a psychiatrist our GP had suggested. He went twice. This man said Niki was 'deeply deluded' and 'wilfully mad' – a contradiction, we thought. He also suggested that I might be similarly afflicted if I had not been lucky enough to organise my disordered world in my novels. I think he meant to be comforting. Niki began to leave suicide notes, in my typewriter, written in lipstick on the bathroom mirror.

He refused to take his medication, the prescribed drugs, which might have banished his demons. One doctor suggested that we should dose his coffee in the morning but neither of us could bear to contemplate such a final betrayal. I tried to blackmail him into taking his pills, saying do this for *our* sake, for *my* sake, look at what you have done to our lives, but he only wept, and talked about the 'real me', his 'good self', who only wanted to look after, protect, his parents, his brother and sister.

He blamed his boarding-school for his illness, one master especially, who had treated him as a favourite until his voice broke. He blamed (naturally) Austen and me. Above all, he blamed the mysterious Nigerians, who had beaten him up and twisted his spinal cord. He was in such agonising pain, it was terrible to see. He was certain there must be a physical cause, a physical cure. Our GP sent him for all the tests she could think of: blood tests, X-rays, a brain scan. As each test came back negative, his despair grew. I was infected by it. I took him to see my old Auntie Aggie in Southend. He was lovely with her; teasing her, flirting a little, making her laugh. But on the way home he was groaning with the incapacitating pain in his belly, begging me to promise that when he died, I would insist on a post-mortem. Driving up the Southend Road, I thought the best thing – the right thing, the only thing – would be to crash the car into the lumbering lorry ahead of us and kill us both; I had brought him into the world, I ought to go with him if he wanted to leave it. Then the cringing awfulness of this high-toned sentiment shamed me. 'Soppy ha'porth,' I muttered under my breath – a put-down from childhood. But I couldn't see the road ahead, I was crying so hard. Niki said, in a normal voice, 'What on earth's the matter, Mum? For heaven's sake stop at the next lay-by or we'll have an accident.'

Danger always alerted him, gathered his splintered self into a purposeful whole. Once, staying with friends for the weekend, a boy fell through a greenhouse roof. Niki organised ambulances, stopped the bleeding, comforted the child. He had always been fine in emergencies; now it was only in emergencies that he was able to act. He understood this himself. He said he wanted to work on an oil rig. He thought he could manage that. He said, if he wasn't dying, that is what he would like to do.

It distressed him that we refused to accept he was dying of some as yet undiscovered disease. We were sympathetic, we knew that his pain was real, not 'just in his head', but we couldn't believe in his physical illness unless we went mad too.

He didn't think he was mad, nor did he want other people to think it. He wanted to be well. He wanted to be ordinary. We had people to dinner and he sat at the table and smiled. When Austen took him to watch him play real tennis at Lord's, Niki put on his suit so he 'wouldn't let him down'. He did the small jobs I invented, and that Jo, our daily help who loved him as we did, found for him. He walked the dog by the canal and sat on a bench, watching the water and smoking. When we flew to Russia for ten days, he went to Sussex to stay with George Hardinge, my publisher, and managed to get there and back on his motor bicycle. In the evenings, the three of us played Scrabble and watched television.

The collapse came suddenly. All at once, he could not go out alone; if his balance failed, he would fall down in the street and the terrible doctors would take him away and abuse him. He began to say he was poisonous. He was afraid of infecting us; he refused to see friends, he refused to see his daughter, whom he loved, in case he should poison her. There was nothing we could do for him; no comfort we could give him. He was beyond our reach now.

Our GP suggested he go to a clinic run by an American doctor, a disciple of R.D. Laing. This man came to see us, accompanied by a monkish acolyte who said nothing, only smiled beatifically. Our GP came to this meeting, and our daughter, but the decision was to be Niki's. He seemed persuaded that this clinic, which the doctor referred to as a 'crisis refuge', could help him. Perhaps he hoped for a miracle. Or simply to get away, to hide in a safe place where he could poison no one, do no more damage.

We talked on the telephone. He said, 'You know, Mum, these people are really *weird*.' We were invited to a 'family therapy' session with the doctor and the acolyte. The doctor asked us what we were doing. I said I was finishing a novel. Austen spoke about his job in the World Service of the BBC. He said he enjoyed it so much that the prospect of retirement was quite disturbing. The American doctor delivered his verdict. We were a couple 'obsessed with death'. I was finishing a novel, Austen thinking about his retirement . . .

Niki and Austen and I exchanged glances. When we were left alone, the three of us collapsed in shared laughter. Niki looked, and sounded, so normal; more normal, certainly, than the doctor and his saintly-seeming acolyte. Until he said, 'They're very polite. They know that I smell bad because my bowels are melting and dropping out, but they pretend not to notice.'

We took him to a pub. We said he must come home if he wanted to – we were afraid to insist, to say that we missed him in case it was true what they said, that our fears and hopes burdened him. He shook his head and smiled. He said, he might as well stay, since the next two weeks had been paid for. (The clinic cost £800 a week and insisted on being paid two weeks in advance.) Niki said, because we had paid for him, not the social services, he was a parlour boarder; he had been given the biggest and the best bedroom. He asked for money. I gave him £20 and he asked for more. That should have warned us. But he said he had had to borrow some money and, as we always did, as we always had done, we believed him.

We walked him back to the clinic when the pub closed, and left him at the gate. We turned back before we got into the car and saw him standing and looking after us, as he used to stand all those years ago, looking after us when we left him at school.

He disappeared three days later. The clinic did not tell us for forty-eight hours. (Although he had telephoned us fairly regularly, we had been asked not to telephone him.) It was the acolyte who rang us, and then only to ask if Niki had friends in Putney. He said Niki had asked him to call a taxi to take him to Putney Bridge.

He had, we realised afterwards, done his best to say goodbye. He had seen his ex-girlfriend and given her all the money he had in his bank account – which was about £100. He had telephoned me and talked for a little about nothing much; he had rung and spoken to several of his friends; he had tried, without success, to reach his sister and his brother. (When Perdita got his message and rang back, she was told by the staff that he had 'gone out for the moment'.) He had left his keys, his wallet and his cheque book on the mantelpiece in his parlour boarder's room. And a poem scrawled in red ink, that began, 'Build a pyre and build it high, and burn the body that was I', and ended, 'God bless you all.'

I went with a friend and found these sad, clear messages. The staff had not checked his room. I screamed at them, accusing them, blaming them for criminal complacency and incompetence. If they had looked in his room earlier, there might have been time to get to Putney, alert the police, *save* him. He didn't want to die, not in his heart, or he would never have told them so expressly where he wanted the taxi to go. Did these idiots not *know* that the river at Putney was exceptionally deep and dangerous?

I was surrounded by bright, sanctimonious faces. No one, clearly, felt the slightest shame. It was against the clinic's policy to enter a guest's room; an important part of the therapy they offered was to ensure that everyone had a private, inviolable space. And it was *morbid* of me to assume the worst; a confirmation of the doctor's judgement that we were obsessed with death.

Against the clinic's wishes, we told the police our son had disappeared. A policeman went to the clinic and the staff confirmed that

Niki had, indeed, 'left' them, but that they believed he had gone to visit friends. The clinic doctor came to see us, bringing his acolyte, for a 'family therapy session'. Perdita came, and the three of us listened in numb amazement as the doctor set out an even more ingenious theory for Niki's troubles than the family interest in death. Niki, he said, had needed to free himself from us all, to escape from us, even if death was the only way. If it turned out that Niki had in fact killed himself, he would consider that the therapy he had been given at the clinic had been a success.

Austen and I could not speak. Perdita, white with rage, said that she wanted a word with the doctor in private. They went downstairs, and although we could hear Perdita's clear, forceful voice from my study on the floor below, we could not make out what she said. It subdued the doctor, however, if only briefly – although he left us with a shamed and mumbled farewell, his bill for the session arrived two days later.

Time was suspended; nothing made sense. It was dark November weather. We knew he was dead, in our hearts; knew that if he were alive he would have telephoned to say he was safe, but everyone seemed to conspire to make us feel we were being morbidly defeatist. He was on the police computer as a missing person but the police made it clear that they would take no further action. It was not their business to chase an adult male of thirty-three who may have simply decided to go away and make a new life for himself. Other people were more helpful: a kind probation officer; the Salvation Army who searched for months, always keeping in touch, ending their letters, *God bless you* – which made me want to cry. Robert decided to believe Niki had joined the Foreign Legion and, as the weeks went by, this seemed to make as much sense as anything.

We bought an answering machine for the times we had to be out of the house. We lay awake at night, listening for his footfall in the street, the knock on the door, the ring of the bell. Every time a taxi stopped outside the house, one of us would be out of bed and at the window in a second, stomach churning. I stood at the bathroom window in the morning and all the men who went past on the canal towpath looked like Niki. He had been wearing an old red leather jacket when he went away and that winter each young man we saw in London, on the pavement, overtaking on his motorbike, seemed to be wearing a leather jacket of exactly the same colour and decrepitude.

In a house in North London, a number of decaying bodies were found in a drain, young men who had been lured to their death by a necrophiliac murderer. We waited for these bodies to be identified, daily expecting a policeman at the door. In the end, the crime writer, Michael Underwood, who had recently retired from the Crown Prosecution Service, suggested that I wrote to the duty officer at Scotland Yard. They might have Niki's details on the computer, Michael said, but a computer is useless unless someone looks at it. I wrote to the duty officer, a detailed letter, and two days later a police inspector from Wapping called on Austen at the BBC to tell him they had taken his son's body from the river the previous December. There had been nothing to identify him, no cheque book, no diary. Eventually they had matched his fingerprints with those on his criminal record; a constable had called at our old house in Weybridge which had been his address when he was sent to prison and the present owners – out of mistaken kindness? – had refused to say where he lived now.

Statistics suggest (if you believe them) that at least one in a hundred of the world's population is schizophrenic and the incidence is the same in remote African villages as in New York or London. Symptoms vary from loss of concentration, withdrawal and apathy, to wilder disorders: catatonia, paranoia, the hearing of voices, delusions of grandeur. In a way, acute sufferers are the more fortunate. Their illness is plain to see, is clearly not idleness or some mysterious failure of will. If Niki had believed he was Napoleon, even our parents would never have suggested that he should 'pull himself together'.

And yet that is precisely what he would have done if he could. But he was too fragmented and confused; as confused as the inadequate net of hospital and community services that promised so much but were unable to deliver the help that he needed. In fact, the failure of the welfare state we had once believed in so innocently, the failure of the supporting services, the outpatient clinics, the social workers, to keep in touch, co-ordinate, communicate with each other, often seemed to be a wicked parody of the illness that plagued him.

The messages that reached Niki from the outside world were hopelessly scrambled. Trying to decipher them exhausted his courage; it was simpler to believe that his body was physically decomposing and stinking, that he was carrying some obscure germ that would poison the people he loved, and so the best thing, the only thing, was to die; to free himself would be to give us our freedom too.

Robert took his motorbike, Perdita his old oak chest, his daughter, Jessica, his poems and his desk. We scattered his ashes round the roots of the *viburnum fragrans* that we had grown from a cutting taken from my Aunt Peg's garden. We kept his African drums and most of his books – he had an impressive collection of books that had been borrowed, over ten or so years, from public libraries in Surrey, Kent and Central London, many of them too badly mildewed to consider their return, even if we had had the energy. A month after the funeral a letter came: he had won £50 on premium bonds. And a friend wrote, 'Now when they ask, *is it well with the child?* you can believe that at last *it is well.*'

We went away that summer and when we came home, turning into our street in Islington, I thought for a moment that I saw him, sitting on a bench in the little park in Colebrooke Row and feeding the fat pigeons at his feet. And, perhaps because I never saw him dead or dying, because the police would not let me see the photographs of his drowned body, I went on seeing him for years. He would be on the motorbike that drew up beside me at a traffic light; turning a street corner too far ahead for me to catch him up; on the top deck of a passing bus.

I still see him. Several days running, a tramp sits on the seat by the canal at the bottom of our garden. I can see him from the bathroom window. He wears a drab, hooded, enveloping garment that he has probably slept in. He usually has a plastic bag with a can of beer in it and a newspaper; he drinks the beer and does the crossword and occasionally looks up at the house.

I know it cannot be Niki, but I find myself trembling. Should I get my binoculars and make sure? Or go and walk past him? Whoever it is looks as if he needs money. Except for the Salvation Army, I no longer give money to charities but for Niki's sake I give on the streets, to the derelict, the homeless, the mad. But I am too late to give this man some beer money. He gets up, shakes the full skirt of his coat, folds his newspaper, tucks the empty can in his pocket. The hood falls back showing a heavy-jowled face with a bulbous nose as warty as a Jerusalem artichoke, and I find myself breathing out, a long sigh of relief. Not just because that sad old tramp is not Niki, but because Niki is safe now. *Is it well with the child? It is well.*

CHAPTER SIX

The Last Barricade

My father died quite unexpectedly one Sunday lunchtime with his second pink gin in his hand. He was in his ninetieth year. A good exit, he would have said – indeed, often *had* said, commending some old friend or other for not 'hanging about' or 'being a burden'. Death was the price you paid for living. What he feared was the process of dying.

I loved my mother – and was a little afraid of her. She was iron-willed and competent in ways that I was not. After she died, Robert said he would always remember his grandmother's useful, determined hands: making pastry, fastening knots in shoelaces, unscrewing jam-jar lids – to the end of her life she had stronger wrists than any other woman I have known.

And, or so it seemed to me, she was without fear. I was afraid of spiders, of big, barking dogs, of the milkman's horse with its white, rolling eye. My mother fed the fat spider that lived above the kitchen sink, tossing dead flies into its dusty web, and she patted the horse on its pale, velvet nose. She tried to persuade me to offer it half an apple on my open palm, but I was too afraid of its teeth – so yellow and slimy and long.

That was when I was young. When I was older, I saw she was brave in other ways, too. My father was at sea all my childhood and my mother was virtually a single parent. She stayed in London throughout the

Blitz and taught at a short-staffed city school until Robin caught diphtheria and nearly died.

I think she was happier in Shropshire than at any other time in her adult life, but when the war ended, and my father retired, she came back to London without complaint. My father's pension, after forty years of service with the P & O company was remarkably mean and when they moved to Kent she started teaching again, in her fifties, so that there should be enough money to send Robin to a good public boarding-school. She remained, in all our eyes, absolutely strong and dependable. One winter, she caught pneumonia and was taken into the cottage hospital; I went to see her and was unreasonably shocked to find her in bed. Oh, she was sitting up, smiling, but sitting up and smiling *in bed*! She said, 'Don't look so shocked, silly girl. I'll be out of here tomorrow.'

My father died in 1976, the same year as her much loved older sister, our tall Aunt Peg who had lived next door to her, and Robin and I persuaded her to move into London. She was seventy-eight then, still physically strong enough to walk several miles and jump on and off buses, and lively-minded enough to make new friends, a new life for herself. She was about eighty-four when she began, very slowly, to be more dependent. She lived two doors away from my brother and his family and a mile away from me. Since I was the only adult able to organise my working life to suit myself, I visited her regularly; three or four times a week to begin with, once a day later on. She had a miniature schnauzer bitch she was devoted to. My brother, or my niece, walked Trinket in the mornings, I exercised her in the afternoons. Then my mother would make tea for me and a slice of toast that was always buttered to the *very edge*. She said, quite rightly, that it was the only way to butter toast. She began to repeat this rather frequently, several times every afternoon. When tea was over, I would fetch the sweet sherry from the corner cupboard, and we would watch *Nationwide* together.

Her other sister died, and Niki, her oldest grandson. And one of her best friends from her teacher-training college. The last of her generation, she said, no one left. But the next day, when I thought she might want to talk about this friend, she had forgotten her name.

She said that sometimes things slipped away. She said that she hoped her memory would 'see her out'. She said she hoped she might see Peter, who was living in Australia, once more before she died.

One day she was very aggrieved. She had jumped off a moving bus with Trinket in her arms. A man had caught her and said, 'You're too old to do that sort of thing at your age, m'darling.' From that day she began to walk like an old woman; chin thrust forward, bent over.

She took Trinket to the vet and had her destroyed. She said it was the only kind thing to do, since she would soon be unable to do anything for her. Afterwards – the next day – she said she thought she must have been mad.

Or prescient. (She had other 'powers', after all; she was a water diviner, and once, standing on the clifftop in Herne Bay, she said she was sure there had been an earthquake somewhere; we heard, on the six o'clock news, that there had been a terrible earthquake in Turkey.) She was taken ill a week later, with acute vomiting and diarrhoea, and in the hospital the surgeon diagnosed a twisted bowel. He said he was sorry, but there was no conservative treatment that could help her and he would have to operate. We didn't understand why he should feel the need to apologise, and he didn't explain. Didn't have time to, perhaps, because at that moment my mother, lying on the trolley, on her way to the operating theatre, launched into a dramatic and comprehensive deathbed farewell – to my brother and his wife, to my husband and me. She had had a wonderful life; she didn't mind dying; we were to tell Peter, in Australia, that she would have waited for him to come if she had been able to; she sent her love to her grandchildren; her love to us all. By the time she had finished, even the surgeon was in tears. (Of course, he knew, as we did not, what the result of the anaesthetic could be.)

When she came round, she didn't know where she was. She knew the four of us, but not our children's names. The young surgeon came and sat beside her on the bed and held her hand and asked her how she felt and said he was delighted that the operation had been such a success. She seized her handbag with her free hand and hit him round the head with it. She said, 'Do you call it a success, young man, to drive an old woman out of her wits?'

Even then, we didn't understand. We told ourselves she was still a bit confused by the anaesthetic; she would be 'herself' in a day or two. A more urgent problem was where she was to go when she left hospital. Her own flat was out of the question; the sister said she needed day and night nursing. I lived on five floors and had no suitable room – that is, no room with a bathroom on the same level. My brother and his wife were both out all day. Anyway, my mother had often said she didn't want to live with either of us; our houses were too inconvenient and too cold.

I was told to see the social worker. She was two hours late for our appointment; when she came she said no one had told her that I was waiting; she hadn't come earlier because most people didn't turn up on time. I smiled, determined not to assume that all social workers were incompetent. This one seemed a pleasant girl, a little vague about appointments perhaps, but apparently eager to be helpful. She had a list of convalescent homes of which one was typical: a Salvation Army hostel on the south coast where patients had to make their own beds and be fit to climb stairs because there was no lift. I said I didn't think that would be very suitable for a woman in her eighties who had just had a major abdominal operation. The young woman seemed surprised. I asked her if she had seen my mother and she shook her head. 'We like to see the families first,' she said.

It was quite a cunning move by the NHS, I thought. Offer only farcical possibilities and any family that is not totally destitute will make their own arrangement. Although when we did so it turned out not much better. We drove my bewildered mother to a highly recommended private nursing home in Wimbledon. They showed us into a room about ten foot by eight which contained two other aged persons. I said, 'My mother has never shared a room with a stranger in her life. I don't think this is a good time to begin.'

The nurse – a sister, or a matron? – smiled. 'You'll learn,' the smile said. She showed us into a narrow single room which was dull but adequate and we waited outside while my mother was helped into bed. When we came into the room she looked at us, terrified and angry, and began to cry. Her distress focused on a dreadful coloured picture on the wall – a picture of a leering and hideous clown. The nurse said, 'Most old people like that picture because it's nice and bright', and I decided that she must be deranged. Or drunk. A kind of Mrs Gamp. What were we doing? Were *we* drunk, or mad?

We took the picture off the wall and put it in the gimcrack wardrobe. My brother and I were as bewildered as my mother by the sudden and unexpected change in her; the headlong decline from powerful adult to shaken and frightened child. My brother wanted to take her home with him immediately. I hesitated. Mrs Gamp, all at once seeming much more kind and sensible, pointed out that my mother was exhausted by the journey and that she needed careful nursing which she hadn't had in hospital. 'You should see the wound,' she said, and clicked her tongue. 'I would never have sent a patient home in that condition from any ward of mine when I was Sister.'

Not only kind and sensible, I decided gratefully, but infinitely more capable than we were. Just a few days here and my mother would be physically stronger, better able to be moved to somewhere more suitable. We lived in Islington, a long way from Wimbledon. Why had we come here?

'Why on earth did we go there?' my brother asked as we drove home. 'It was what we could afford,' I said. 'Well,' he said, 'she can't stay there.' Guilt made us out of temper with each other.

After five days, Robin took her home with him. He had enough room; a wife and three growing children who were fond of her; a mother-in-law who was a saint. I would go in for part of every day, and we would employ what other help seemed needed. My mother was pleased to be there to begin with. But she grew increasingly suspicious; whenever we went out of the room she thought we were plotting against her. We were sure that this was bound to change as she recovered and her memory improved. We still innocently believed that all that was needed to mend her poor mind was love and care and familiar people round her.

We asked if she felt well enough to go back to her flat; there was a woman who had helped her in the house who was willing to move in and look after her. My mother became very agitated. She announced that she wished to go into a home, 'where she could be looked after properly'. This was a decision entirely in character – in spite of her increasing dementia, her personality seemed quite unchanged. She had always had a kind of impatient courage that not only met life head on, but made her go forward to meet it. If a home and professional care was inevitable, better sooner rather than later. 'If it's got to be, it's best to get it over with,' she said. 'I'd like to get it off my mind.'

We looked at a number of what seemed to us terrible places. There was a home on the fringes of London where the inmates (known as 'guests') were watched through a television monitor. And at another, the nurse who was showing us round suddenly flung open a door, gestured at an old man lying in bed, his bony nose pointing at the ceiling, and said, with a bright, conspiratorial leer, 'You can see this room's likely to be vacant by the end of the week.' Eventually we settled on a half-private, half-charitable institution in north London, beguiled by a pretty, youngish, rather gushing matron, fresh flowers in the hall, and a smell of polish instead of disinfectant.

We took my mother there. She said, accusingly, when we were being shown around the garden, 'Where are all the happy old ladies laughing and talking under the chestnut tree?', and we knew that we had failed her. Leaving her there was like abandoning a child to strangers. A hurt and angry child. And, as if she were speaking about a child, the pretty matron said, 'Don't worry, she'll settle down once you've gone. But don't come too often for the first week or two, let her get used to us.'

This home did not, as a policy, admit people with senile dementia. My mother had a sense of propriety and a good social manner which had concealed her true condition from us, from the matron, and even, for a while, from the sympathetic doctor who had examined her. But her co-prisoners were sharper. Scenting in my mother the weakness that they feared lay in wait for them around the next corner, they turned on her like savage children. They hid her handbag. They whispered amongst themselves when she came into a room and they laughed at her when she turned her back to leave. Driven to despair she telephoned the four of us in turn, sometimes weeping, sometimes raving like a lunatic. She wrote scrawling, frantic, accusing letters. Were we quite heartless? She had taken care of us, had we no thought for her, no room in our lives, no chimney corner? It was painful and frightening for us. It must have been much worse for her.

She refused to eat. I found jam sandwiches hidden in her shoes. She said they were trying to poison her. Then she had a fall and was taken to hospital. The X-ray showed nothing. But she was crying with the pain; insisting she couldn't stand up, couldn't get off the bed. The matron said, 'She is trying to get attention. She is a manipulative woman, your mother.'

I said, 'She's in pain. Anyone can see she's in pain.'

We told her doctor that we wanted a second opinion. There was no point in sending her back to the hospital where they had found nothing wrong. A geriatric psychiatrist came to visit her; a careful, concerned woman who comforted us all. She admitted my mother to an acute psychiatric unit; a pleasant, old-fashioned, rambling building near Highgate Woods. She was X-rayed again, more carefully, and found to have a crush fracture of the spine which must, the psychiatrist said, have been agonising. They treated the injury, coaxed her to walk again and, with what seemed to us miraculous skill, managed to calm her agony of mind. They played card games and word games with her, and were delighted when she won at Scrabble. When they had time, they took her to the woods in a wheelchair; they washed her hair and did her nails, treating her always with respect and dignity. It became a pleasure to visit her. I took Niki's daughter to see her and she was a smiling great-grandmother, a bit forgetful, but asking the right questions about school, boyfriends and going to university.

They couldn't keep her for ever. This was an acute unit; she had already stayed longer than the NHS rules allowed. After three months we must find somewhere else for her. But the unit would help us to make the decision; she would spend a day in each place we suggested, and a nurse would go and spend the day with her and see how she reacted. 'She might have a little trouble remembering how she really felt otherwise,' they said tactfully.

The nurse was a tall young man my mother was especially fond of. He insisted that she appeared not only to understand the choice she was making but also that it was Hobson's choice; that nowhere could be perfect. They settled on a large home run by Islington Council with an exceptionally sensitive and energetic matron, small but decent rooms and – something that seemed to me important – an always open office where the residents could wander in at will to talk to the matron, or to get lights for their cigarettes, stamps for their letters.

Although my mother wept when she left the unit, kissing the nurses and thanking them, saying, 'My dears, I have been so happy here', she was not *unhappy* in her new home. Or, rather, when she was unhappy, she never told Robin or me. She once said to Austen, who was taking her along the corridor to her room after a day spent with us, 'Oh, Austen, I don't like it here, but you mustn't tell Nina or Robin.' But the rage and despair she had felt to begin with seemed to fade as her memory faded; as her grasp on reality loosened.

I was sitting with her in her little room one winter afternoon. She said, 'What's outside this room, Nina? I know I ought to know, but I can't remember.' I described the long, bare corridor that she didn't much care for, the lift at the end, the dining room that would be laid now for supper, the large living room with the television and the awful plastic daffodils. She nodded. She said, 'I believe you. But it seems to me that we are sitting here alone, in a small, bright capsule, spinning through the dark.' And she said to Austen, when he picked her up on Easter Sunday, 'It seems dreadful, but I have forgotten what Easter is *for*. Though I know it is something important.'

She never forgot us. And she remembered the children's names now. She knew Niki was dead, and spoke of him lovingly. She knew that Robert was a doctor and that Perdita was in the theatre and that my brother's children were all still at school. But when Perdita had a baby and we took my mother to the hospital, she cuddled the tiny, swaddled girl – who had been brought out of an incubator to meet her great-grandmother – and said, 'Is it *mine*?' We reassured her and she seemed relieved. She said, 'How clever of you, Perdita.' We beamed; we thought Perdita was clever, too. But this was not what my mother meant. The maternity ward at St Bartholomew's Hospital was full of visiting fathers. Husbands. My mother looked at them with contempt and said, very loudly and clearly, 'So clever to get a baby without having to put up with one of *those.*'

We went away for three months. It had been planned long ago. I telephoned from abroad and was told she was well. Coming back, I was nervous. How could I have left her so long? But when we walked in, Austen and I, she looked at us smiling. 'How lovely to see you, how good of you to come again so soon, you were only here yesterday.'

But she was helpless. That is the thing I remember. This strong, brave woman who had been used all her life to running her own affairs, making decisions for herself and for others, was at the mercy of people who might be kind most of the time but could be insensitive, lazy, forgetful. She was deaf; she was always losing her hearing aid. Or it needed a battery. She couldn't read the newspaper or a letter. It was a while before we found out that she had been given new glasses but they were only for distance. She had never worn distance glasses and didn't understand why she couldn't read with them. And there was the tyranny of enforced entertainment. And worse! One Friday I found the big living room invaded by a strident horde of hellfire alarmists from an enthusiastic local church; a preacher waving his arms about, threatening the innocent souls in his captive audience with eternal damnation, and a pianist thumping out the accompaniment to noisy hymns of a violent nature.

My mother was looking bemused. I took her away, and we sat outside the entrance, on the bench where the old men went to smoke, cigarette stubs round our feet. I thought of complaining to Islington Council, a leftish regime that would be hard pressed to make the proper reaction. They would naturally be against thrusting religion down the throats of these defenceless, elderly people. But then, consider! These fundamentalists were black. It might be racist to object to them . . .

The hellfires came out of the home at the same moment that a group of Hasidim passed by; men with skullcaps and beards, little boys with long ringlets, on their way to synagogue. We watched as the two groups met on the pavement. They didn't look at each other, not one glance, not a single eye contact, but they parted smoothly, each allowing the other to pass through their midst without hindrance. 'Like the Red Sea,' my mother said, and laughed.

She had trouble breathing one night. The night staff called an ambulance. They telephoned us and we went to the Whittington hospital. We found the casualty department in uproar. I think it was a Saturday night. No one seemed to have heard of my mother. At last we found her behind a flowered curtain, trying to get off a trolley; a young woman doctor wrestling with her, shouting at her. She said, to us, 'How can I take a history from this old woman if she refuses to tell me what's wrong with her?' She was blazing with fury – exhaustion too, probably, but in the circumstances that did not seem much mitigation. We pointed out that my mother was senile. I said, 'It happened here, in this hospital, it was the anaesthetic.' She turned her rage – and her weary frustration – on me. 'Do you mean you are *blaming the hospital?*' My mother said, 'Oh, Nina, I'm glad you've come, would you explain to this angry girl that I'm not trying to escape, that I just want to go to the lavatory?'

She died in another hospital. She had pneumonia. It was a terminal ward, glittery with Christmas decorations. We went to see her on Christmas morning. We were not the first visitors. The mayor and his male companion had been to the ward, taken presents, given each patient a card, signed by both of them. Their relationship, the sister said, had puzzled some of the older ladies. We gave my mother a necklace of ceramic beads and she held it to her face, trying to look at it. Her hands moved very slowly and her eyes looked different; greener than usual, and shining, but somehow unseeing. Although her face had colour, the flesh seemed to have shrunk away from her cheekbones since we had seen her the evening before. I said, 'I wish you were having Christmas dinner with us, Mum, instead of in this mouldy old hospital,' and found myself choking on tears. She said, sounding quite strong and cheerful, 'I shall enjoy thinking about you all but I'm a good deal more comfortable here.'

They telephoned from the hospital while Robin was carrying in the flaming Christmas pudding. When we got to the ward, the doctor and the staff nurse had whisky and tea waiting for us. One of them told me that she had been sitting beside her bed, sipping her Christmas glass of red wine, when she suddenly shouted, 'I'm finished!' She had always had a good sense of theatre.

A tumour in her lung had burst. It was a mercy; they would have had to put her through painful tests to discover the nature of the cancer that killed her. I said, angrily, 'But she never smoked in her life,' and the doctor said, gently, 'She was old, dear, it sometimes happens when people are old.' It is often very soothing, the comfort of strangers.

We drank our tea and whisky and went home. We drew the curtains to darken the room; Robin lit the pudding again and we ate it with brandy butter. We pulled the crackers with the children. I thought – well, this is what it is like. Pieces of yourself fall away. When Niki had died, when the police found him in the river, it had been a visceral pain; a disembowelment. This, my mother's death, was different, more like losing part of one's life rather than part of one's body; a link broken with the past, with a long-ago childhood. I remember my babies when they were born, exactly how they looked, each of them, the first time I saw them. No one now to remember me; no one to call me a 'silly girl', or to say, 'Trust you, Nina!' Or, 'Nina, you *would*!'

I said, incompetently helping to clear up in the kitchen, 'Robin, d'you know what? We are orphans now.'

There were odds and ends of her life to be tidied away. I took a black bin bag of old clothes from the home and the hospital, and found the pathos of the things she had left behind almost unbearable. There was a watch we had bought her with a big, clear face, Roman numerals, but it was broken. There were some pieces of jewellery. The furniture from her flat, crockery, books, none of these things had the throat-catching impact of something she had worn: a blouse she had been fond of, a pair of shabby slippers . . .

I had been about ten. I had come home from school and her shoes were steaming in front of the fire. She was wearing slippers. She said, 'I got caught in the rain,' and turned the shoes over to get the heat to the soles. There were holes the size of a penny. I said, 'You ought to get your shoes mended,' and she laughed. She said, 'They're the only shoes I've got, silly girl.'

I remembered how little she took for herself. My father was seldom at home; she hardly ever went out – to a cinema, a play, or a party. My father was anxious about money. My mother may have worried too but if she did she never showed it. It was not until after my father retired that she had a proper holiday with him; they went to Ireland with friends, to New Guinea to see Peter.

Guilt flooded in, self-indulgent, as guilt always is. There was the day she had telephoned me to say there were white horses and a band on Highbury Fields, a celebration for May Day, and I had said, no, I couldn't come now, I wanted to finish writing my chapter. And another time, further back, just before Perdita was born, when she had travelled from Kent to look after the boys and help with the new baby. She came, looking cold and tired; she had had a long, chilly train journey, from Kent, across London, to Surrey. I was doing the ironing and didn't stop until I had finished it, not to make her a cup of tea or even to kiss her. And, of course, above all, I should never have left her to die alone in the hospital.

There were almost certainly other occasions, but these are the ones I remember.

I was at a loss in the afternoons now, without occupation. Once, between three o'clock and six, I had thought I had too much to do. I had wrenched myself away from my computer, from my oh-so-important 'work', to walk my mother's stupid, elderly dog, be given tea and toast, drink the sweet sherry (which I didn't much care for) while we watched *Nationwide*. Now those hours stretched out, grey and listless with boredom. There seemed no way of filling them. Unless someone came to see me, I lay on my bed in a kind of stupor, trying to go to sleep, to make the time pass until Austen came home. Or we went out to dinner. I had felt like this after Niki had died four years earlier; the late afternoon was his low point of the day and we would go for a walk, or to the cinema. I had got through that, I told myself; this should be easier. A parent's death is part of life; a natural progression. Leaving their children on the last barricade. Among the grown-ups at last.

I did other things in the late afternoons. Now, only a kind of nostalgic sadness touches me sometimes; around five o'clock in the summer, earlier in the winter, when it begins to get dark. I think, I should have looked after them better. Both my son and my mother. I know better now about old age, the falling away, the senility. But there are no second chances.

Sometimes I catch myself in the mirror, looking a bit like my mother. Pursing my mouth as she did when she was concentrating on something. Talking to myself the way she did occasionally, when she thought she was alone. A fussy little whisper, or mutter. I used to think she was making plans, plotting; now I think she may have been talking to someone she didn't see any longer but suspected might be lurking somewhere quite close, around the next corner.

CHAPTER SEVEN

Speaking for Myself

'Why don't you write a novel like *The Caine Mutiny?*' my father said, one summer evening in his great old age, leaning back in his chair with his pipe in his mouth and his beret on the back of his bald head to keep off the draught from the window behind him.

He had read very little before he left the sea but since then he had gone – or, to be more exact, sent my mother – to the public library two or three times a week. Retiring at sixty-three, and now in his ninetieth year, he had been blessed with almost a third of his life to catch up on his reading. He read mainly history, or political memoirs, rarely novels. But he had read *The Caine Mutiny* and enjoyed it more, I suspect, than he had ever enjoyed any novel of mine.

A small boy once asked me, bringing a children's book for my signature at some book fair or other, if I had 'ever thought of writing like Shakespeare'. My father's equally innocent question was harder to answer. I said (honestly) that a writer can't choose the voice that she writes in, and (more dubiously) that I didn't have the right kind of experience. In fact, I was flustered. I never really knew my father until he was old, and had never learned how to talk to him about something that mattered to me. Now I tried, but made a mess of it, trying out arguments that sounded specious even as I ventured them. I lectured him on my pitiful situation as a married woman. How could I write 'adventure stories about the sea' – consoling myself for a fancied slight by thus snidely pigeon-holding *The Caine Mutiny* –

when I was stuck at home with housework and children? Of course anything I wrote was bound to be domestic, and family centred because that was all that I *knew*. I had to work with what lay to hand. And I didn't think, *personally* that to write social comedies was such a trivial matter. Jane Austen, after all . . .

My father leaned forward with a grunt of effort, emptied his pipe in his brass ashtray and regarded the bowl. He said, 'Your first novel was about a murderer who had a twin sister with a wooden leg. Bit of imagination at work there, I thought.'

I wrote about my father in *Walking Naked*. Or, rather, since he was dead by the time I was writing that novel, I wrote about how I remembered him, selecting the bits and pieces of his character and appearance and history that suited the story I was trying to tell. I had made use of him before in a much earlier novel, disguising him as an elderly chiropodist, but as is usually the case in a straightforward theft of this kind, he hadn't noticed. Perhaps he had not recognised himself because the chiropodist was a peripheral character, of no great importance to the plot, and it would not have occurred to my father, who had a reasonable conceit of himself, that I might have 'put him in a book' to play such a minor role. The truth is, central characters are usually too complex to be taken directly from life. You can only guess at what 'real' people think and feel but in fiction you have to know – which means to make up, imagine, put yourself in their place. And, as my father reminded me, when I wrote my first novel I knew no murderers, no beautiful and wicked girls with wooden legs. I didn't know much about anything.

I was aware of my ignorance. I was really quite humble. I was sure I had nothing to say that would be of interest to anyone. I had lived through a war but only at second hand, on the edge of things; I had not been a fighter pilot, or a merchant seaman, or even an air-raid warden. To write as if I had been some sort of hero or heroine, a soldier, a sailor, an airman (and how else could one write, to take the war *seriously?*) seemed a kind of impertinence, a shocking presumption on the part of someone who had sat out the war more or less safely in South Wales and Oxford.

That I should write in the first person as a man who was an incestuous murderer may not seem the obvious solution but it was an excellent disguise for a timid writer, frightened that her own voice might sound too presumptuous. And the detective story, or crime novel, which was what I advanced upon in *Who Calls the Tune*, provided a kind of climbing frame within which I could write about the things that interested me: the complexity of motive behind quite simple actions, the difference between what people say and what they actually mean, and the way that a violent event, murder or some other catastrophe, will shock them into showing who they really are.

The fact that I knew nothing about murder or incest or, indeed, dangerous or deviant behaviour of any kind, did not deter me. I had sat in the public gallery at the Old Bailey, met one or two 'spivs' in a 'shady drinking club' in London, and these experiences, together with a devotion to the novels of Graham Greene, gave me the assurance to tackle the underworld. Julian Symons, who included my second crime novel, *The Odd Flamingo*, in his choice of twelve novels reprinted by Collins to mark their Crime Club's Golden Jubilee, said in his introduction that my fascination with crime and criminals came through but it was the fascination of 'a sinister fairy tale rather than of grubby actuality', which is very fair comment. And Maurice Richardson, reviewing it in the *Observer*, suggested that my 'doom-laden puddings could do with a pinch of salt' – a piece of advice that I took to heart as I grew older and more confident.

My first novel, however, was very nearly my last. This was the one about the relationship between a pair of incestuous twins, one of whom had a wooden leg and was found murdered fairly early on in the novel. There was also a character based on William Joyce (Lord Haw-Haw, who was hanged after the war for his propaganda broadcasts from Germany) and a delicate but depraved German girl who was his lover. The narrator was the male twin, who was modelled partly on Humphrey Bogart and partly on the narrator of one of Graham Greene's gloomier works, *The End of the Affair*.

It was a good, frightening story. Indeed, it had quite frightened me as I wrote it – telling no one what I was doing in case they should laugh at me. Although I had every intention of sending it to a publisher when it was finished, I had not allowed myself to think beyond packing it up in strong brown paper and sending it to Collins Crime Club. And when I needed a German name for the mistress of the William Joyce character, I reached back into memory, found a name, took it, and thought no more about it. By the time the book was finished I had forgotten what I had done.

And then, almost immediately, I was caught up in a heady storm of excitement. I had a letter from George Hardinge at Collins. He asked me to come to see him. I arranged for someone to look after the baby and caught the train to London. I walked from Waterloo to St James's on rubbery legs. When George (very tall, and young, and dashingly romantic in his general presence) said that he wanted to publish my novel, I thought I would faint with joy and terror. I suppose I spoke, at least answered the questions I was asked. Then Billy Collins was suddenly there, beaming benevolently. 'So this is the new find, is it? What is she doing for lunch?' (It is my recollection that he spoke of me in the third person, but I was so overwhelmed by the alarming glamour of this occasion that my memory may have faltered.)

But I do remember my answer. I said that I would love to have lunch, it was just unfortunate that I had a dentist's appointment. I was afraid that my blushes would expose this cowardly lie, but both men appeared to accept it quite calmly. As I left, I wondered why I had been so foolish and craven. It wasn't just that I feared the invitation had been mere politeness, or that I wouldn't know what to talk about. The truth was that the excitement of being a published author, if only in prospect, was almost too much to bear. I needed to be alone with it, to get used to it, not subdue it, pretend that it was an everyday matter to me, as I assumed I would have to do were I to lunch with two such grown-up and sophisticated men. (I was still, instinctively, and entirely respectfully, marking the gulf between people who had been old enough for the war and those of us who had been too young to fight. In fact, although Billy Collins was middle-aged then, George Hardinge, though an ex-naval officer, was still in his twenties, only a few years older than me.)

I got a seventy-five pounds' advance for *Who Calls the Tune*, half on signature, half on publication. This was a good advance in the early

1950s for a first novel. It came out to astonishingly good reviews and it seemed to me that life could hold no more happiness without bursting. And then, one morning, I had a letter from my old head-mistress.

She wrote, not to congratulate me, but to complain. I had 'used' the name of one of the Jewish girls who had been rescued from Europe just before the war to be educated at my grammar school, for one of my 'disreputable characters'. The girl herself would probably be spared distress as she was now married and living in Germany and unlikely to come across my book, but what about the people who had funded her throughout the war? How would they feel, to see the girl they had supported so generously depicted as 'a loose woman and a murder suspect'? What was I going to do about it? How could I make amends?

My first reaction was bewilderment. I was so sure of my own innocent intention that I managed to persuade myself it was all a preposterous fuss about nothing. But when I telephoned George Hardinge, he took it more seriously.

He sent me to his firm's libel lawyers, Goodman and Mann. Arnold Goodman (not yet ennobled) rose stoutly behind his large desk to greet me. 'Ah,' he said, extending his hand, 'you must be my little libel.'

I received this jocularity in the spirit in which it was meant and felt slightly less nervous. I was offered a gin and tonic, which I accepted gratefully. Mr Goodman then sat back in his chair as if he had all the time in the world to spare for me, and entertained me with accounts of a number of literary libels, including one notable case of a well-known lady novelist who had written a novel set in what she claimed was an entirely fictional village in the south of England. Her publishers, suspecting that she might be deluded if not actually lying, called in their lawyers, who employed Hartley Shawcross to question her. Even the ex-Attorney-General was unable to shake her fixed belief that her novel was entirely a work of imagination. But when the book came out, thirty writs for libel were received within the first fortnight.

I laughed, and Arnold Goodman looked pleased. 'So you see,' he said, 'libel is a tricky business. Now tell me about yours.'

He listened attentively; his bloodhound features thoughtful and gloomy. When I had finished, he smiled at me. Then summoned his secretary.

He was still smiling – perhaps with a certain amount of anticipatory glee. He said, 'I am going to dictate a letter for you to send to your old headmistress.'

I sat back comfortably in my chair to finish my gin. I was safe with this large and competent man. He would know exactly what to say to my headmistress, Miss Bull. I felt grateful to him, and grateful to George who had sent me here. I was so deep in gratitude that I was slow to realise the full horror of the letter Arnold Goodman was dictating.

I cannot recall it in full, only a few creepy-crawly phrases like, 'I am so unhappy to think that I have caused distress to someone I honour as I do you'. And, 'You know I would never, intentionally, let down my old school.' But I remember with dreadful clarity the simpering, goody-goody *tone* which I found degrading. I wailed in despair. 'I can't write that sort of letter. Honestly. She wouldn't believe it anyway. I mean, she knows I'm not *like* that. Sucking up to people just so they'll let me off! It's humiliating.'

He said, patiently, 'Do you want a career as a writer? If you were to be sued for libel you would find it harder to get a publisher for your second novel. It's up to you, though.'

He smiled at me kindly. 'You may change my grammar and my syntax if you like, or any word that you find especially tasteless, but the essence of that letter must go. Just remember, a soft answer turns away wrath. Or, in more direct language, people will accept any amount of mush if it is what they want to hear.'

I didn't believe him. But of course he was right. I copied out the letter, hot with shame. And my old headmistress replied by return of post. A loving and forgiving letter. 'Dear Nina . . . I knew you would never deliberately do anything malicious or unkind.'

It was the first time I had understood that even clever people could be manipulated by the sly use of nicely judged sentimentality and it shamed me. It also made me feel genuinely sorry. I turned down an amazingly generous paperback offer. The offending name could have been changed, but to let the novel go out of print seemed the only redress I could make.

I have been careful about names ever since. I find names for my characters on tombstones in country churchyards and in obituary columns. I am suspicious of names that surface from some hidden depth in the mind and offer themselves without effort on my part. Naming a character in a novel is like naming a child – call a boy baby Henry, and almost immediately, in the course of a week or so anyway, he will *become* Henry, drawing on the name like a cloak and making it his alone. The process is the same in fiction, which makes it hard for a novelist to understand how and why people can claim to 'see themselves' in a novel, let alone imagine they have been defamed. If I were to name two characters *Robert* and *Perdita* there might be a brief transitional period in which there were resemblances in my mind between those fictional persons and my son and daughter, mannerisms, tricks of speech, but then the new characters would begin to develop independently, become people in their own right.

I was once invited to attend a seminar in North America where my work for children was being discussed. A bearded professor read a paper about feminism in the Bawden canon. He spoke about the strong, determined women in *The Peppermint Pig*, and then mounted what seemed to me an outrageous attack on the absent father in that novel, who had lost his coach painter's job, gone to America to make his fortune and, of necessity, left his family behind. The professor accused him of being a 'typically uncaring Victorian male'. My stomach churned with indignation. I leapt to my feet and defended my character passionately. Everyone listened politely. When I had finished, there was a silence. Then someone said, 'You talk as if he was a real person.'

Well, he *was* real to me, much more real than the grandfather on whom he was based, the grandfather who died when I was eight. I suppose if he had still been alive when my novel was published, he might have objected to what he might have seen as my portrayal of him, but wrongly, to my mind.

If this sounds disingenuous, a plea for writers faced with the harshness of our libel laws, I can only say it is how it seems to me and, I would think, to all storytellers. Fictional characters have their own lives. They can move and speak in ways their authors may never have intended – or may not have acknowledged, even if they understood how it was done. The sleeping mind is as active as the wakeful one, and often more inventive; reality grows out of dreams and the unconscious mind is a useful tool of any writer's trade.

As is a sense of place. It is important to me to have a clear picture in my mind of the physical setting of a story. I need to know the streets my characters walk down, the kind of houses they inhabit. Some novelists are able to write about exotic places they have never visited; building up a convincing picture of China or Peru from other people's books, railway timetables and travel brochures. I can see how it is done, but it doesn't work for me; even if the background is of only marginal importance, it has to be a place I know, a place of which I have some sensory or tactile memory.

I remember the smells and sounds of Africa. I went to Kenya in the early 1960s to visit Robin, who was a district officer in Kisii just before independence, *Uhuru*, spent a magical month falling in love with Africa and Africans and wrote a novel about the confused attitude of middle-class liberals to their black friends which might seem dated and quaint nowadays, but was true of that time. And a long trip Austen and I made to Turkey in the early 1970s was the springboard for *George beneath a Paper Moon*, which is a story about a travel agent who gets out of his depth in that beautiful, intriguing, and sometimes dangerous country.

I had been to Turkey before and Austen, who was then Head of the South European Service of the BBC, made regular visits to Greece and Turkey, but on this occasion we were on an extended holiday and able to travel more widely. We had Turkish friends who travelled with us and one of them told us a terrible story. He had a young girl cousin whose father was in the Diplomatic Service in South America. She had intended to go to university in the States but after she came back from a holiday in Europe the previous summer, she had told her parents she would rather finish her education at home in Turkey. Since she had an aunt and uncle in Istanbul this was easy to arrange. The autumn and the spring terms passed uneventfully. In the summer, like other comfortably off Turkish families, the aunt and uncle moved out of the heat and pollution of the city to their house on the Bosporus. They assumed that the girl would go with them, but she refused. She would be safe, she said, alone in the apartment in Istanbul.

Her uncle telephoned her parents, who were amused at what they saw as his old-fashioned concern. Their daughter had been brought up in the modern way; unlike most Turkish girls, she had travelled abroad on her own, and was used to looking after herself. Reluctantly, the uncle and aunt left their niece behind in the city. The next time they heard of her, she had been picked up by the police on the Asian side of the Bosporus. She had a heavy trunk with her. She had told the police it was full of books but when they forced the lid open there was a dead man inside.

This was the story she told the police. The man was an acquaintance from the university. He had come to the apartment the previous night and asked for shelter, telling her that the Army were after him. The girl had said he could stay the rest of the night but he would have to leave the next day. Then in the early hours of the morning he came into her room and tried to rape her. That was when she shot him, she said. She took her uncle's gun and shot him to defend her honour.

The police sent for a doctor to examine her. The doctor found that she was not a virgin – which in the eyes of the Turkish police meant that she had no honour to defend and had therefore lied to them. At a time in Turkey, when students were sent to prison for owning a copy of *Das Kapital*, she must have known she could expect little mercy. Fortunately the weather was hot and the window in the security block had been left open. She jumped, broke her back, and was dead before she arrived at the hospital.

The truth, pieced slowly together by our Turkish friend and his dead cousin's parents was, of course, different. The girl was a member of a terrorist organisation. She had been recruited when her innocent parents had sent her to Europe on holiday; instead of sight-seeing, she had gone to East Berlin to be indoctrinated and trained. She had been ordered to go to university in Istanbul and wait for further instructions, but none had been given her until the night of the shooting, when two men came to the apartment and one of them shot the other. It was a disciplinary action; the murdered man had disobeyed an order and paid with his life. His body was put in the trunk and the girl told to call a taxi and take it to the other side of the Bosporus where someone would meet her.

She did as she was told, but the taxi driver was suspicious because the trunk was so heavy. Although he took her in the ferry across the Bosporus, he refused to go further, to the place where she was due to be met (which was some way along on the Asian side, in a paved, pic-nicking area overlooking the river), unless she opened the trunk to show him there really were books inside, as she had told him, and not guns that she was illegally carrying. She said that the books belonged to another student and she had no key. The driver dumped both her and the trunk at the side of the road, and alerted the police when he got back to the Bosporus and the ferry.

A grotesque tale – to English ears. We heard it in Istanbul, from the lips of a civilised, widely read and cultivated man, an honourable member of the government, who had nephews and nieces in prison for terrorist actions. *Wayward children*, he called them. In England they would have been joining protest marches and organising sit-ins at their universities. The situation in Turkey was different. Rebellion was more violent there. And was put down more violently.

I was fascinated by danger, whether natural hazard or political threat. In Turkey at that time no one was immune. Yasar Kemal, the great Turkish novelist, and others less notable, went in and out of prison as a normal part of life. ('Is Yasar in or out?' you asked, the first question on landing in Istanbul.) After a few weeks in Turkey, travelling, listening, my belief in my own safe existence began to seem absurd. Nothing ever happened to me: the great, burning world swept on its passionate and catastrophic way, earthquakes and wars and famines, while I sat on the edge of it, watching. I itched to write about this world that I found so absorbing but had no real part in, that I could never belong to or comprehend from the inside, and a man called George Hare appeared in my mind in the mental equivalent of a puff of smoke. The smoke cleared and he stood there: tall, blond, middle thirties, sweet, bony face. Hare's Travel – Swift and Sure. George was to be an eccentric but successful travel agent, operating in the early days of the package holiday and making a fortune. A natural tourist himself, a looker-on, an outsider, destined always to skim over the surface, a perpetual traveller, but I planned for events, public and private, to catch up with him in Ataturk's famous *hamam* in Bursa.

I had been to Bursa (where you can eat the best kebabs in Turkey) and swum in the hot, steely water of the great *hamam* and seen the bricks of the dome move above me. There had been a small earthquake. The safest place was a *hamam*, someone explained to me; something to do with the way these old Turkish baths were built, not the height, but the curve of the dome. The earthquake I arranged for George was more dramatic but I had seen what *could* happen. And I had spent long enough in the country to understand something of what was happening there, to hear some more stories, to discover that at certain times of the year daphne bushes, in Turkey, smell like ginger cake.

I wrote this novel about Turkey in the early seventies, almost immediately after I had been there. Re-reading it twenty years later, I remember other things besides the smell of ginger cake. I think I caught the politics of that time, the confusion and danger at the heart of ordinary, everyday living. If a novel touches actual events, it becomes history. In *George Beneath a Paper Moon* the history, the social and political background, was something I had to work at, make sure was accurate – and I was lucky to have Turkish friends and a husband in the World Service. In a story set in England, the sense of place is something I can rely on without effort. Without leaving my chair I can move myself back in time, slipping between middle life and childhood and back again between one breath and another, half a century in a split second.

*

In the 1950s my parents retired to Herne Bay, in Kent, to a comfortable house next door to my mother's sister, my Aunt Peg, who had lived there since the thirties with her lifelong friend, another art and drama teacher, called Betty. Peg and Bet, 'the girls', my father called them, were devoted, and complementary; one took care of the garden and grew the vegetables, the other cooked, and cleaned the house. (One of my sons, growing up in the 1960s, once called them 'a sweet, old lesbian couple' and when I tried to explain that although their sexual orientation was a matter of indifference to me, the truth was – I would stake my life on it – that they were simply two women who, given the shortage of men after the First World War had elected to buy a house and make a life together and that they probably didn't even know what the word *lesbian* meant, he merely smiled, as if he knew better.)

I had stayed with Peg and Bet as a child in the 1930s. Now, in the fifties and sixties, when I took my own children to stay with my parents, Peg's house still smelled of childhood for me: of Wright's Coal Tar soap, of the turps she kept to clean her artist's brushes and, above all, of the sweetish smell of leaking gas. When electricity was installed in Peg's house, I missed the smell and the lovely popping sound as the gas mantles were lit.

My children played on the shelving pebble beach and flew kites on the cropped grass of the Downs above the town. There was a good view of the pier from the Downs, and of a bubbling yellow line far out at sea that Aunt Peg said was sewage. From the highest point of the Downs, a wooden stairway, the 'Hundred Steps', descended to an empty shingle beach where iron spikes, relics of the war, lifted their rusty tips above the hissing sea. Bare brown cliffs reared above the shore, hollowed out by high tides, and capped with a narrow frill of grass on the sinister overhang like green icing on a chocolate cake. These cliffs were treacherous; slabs of soft clay could collapse without warning. Houses that were safely inland one summer were teetering on the edge by the next. One winter an entire garden was neatly lopped from its bungalow and fell two hundred feet. In the summer it was still there just as it had fallen: dahlias still flowering, an ornamental pond still intact, a garden gnome still fishing beside it.

There is no land between Herne Bay and the North Pole which is why, between the wars, the air was considered exceptionally healthy; invalids were sent there to recover from TB and pneumonia. The cold wind from the sea flapped the deckchairs on the front and cracked the flags on the roof of the bandstand which had been built, like the clock tower and the handsomely decorated public lavatories, at a time when it was hoped that Herne Bay would become a rival to Brighton and attract 'a better class of person' than the visitors to Birchington or Margate. But by the 1950s it was clear that this was a lost cause. There were no grand hotels, and once away from the pier and the bandstand, the promenade came to an abrupt end, as if the builders had unexpectedly run out of materials, or had simply lost heart.

Herne Bay was in decline along with seaside landladies, Punch and Judy, cafés with faded notices offering 'Oysters in Season'. But seedy places have a perverse attraction, and Herne Bay had great charm for us. There were coloured stones to be searched for among the shingle, steamers passing on the horizon, and we were addicted to the seaweedy smell of estuary mud. We took the children to Dreamland at Margate at least once every holiday, and every week Uncle Jack (or Uncle John, or Uncle Bill) gave a children's entertainment consisting of magic tricks, comic patter, and a Children's Talent Competition, in the bandstand.

It was at Uncle Jack's that we lost our younger son. It was a fitful summer day and the bandstand, though open at the top, was sunny and windless in the sheltered well. The audience was made up of the very young and the very old; the children in the front rows of chairs, the old people, issued with cheap season tickets by the council at the back, beyond the aisle. We – Austen and I – stood at the side where we could just see our boys' blond heads.

They watched Uncle Jack's magic tricks, apparently spellbound. We had no television and they had not seen a conjuror before. It was not until the Talent Competition that Robert, who was only four, grew restive and squirmed round in his seat. We waved and smiled but he didn't seem to see us. Perhaps he wasn't looking for us, anyway. The Talent Competition was soon over and the prizes were presented: ten shillings and five shillings for the first and second prize, and an ice-cream cornet for each competitor.

The pensioners were the first to leave. They got up slowly, stretching aching legs and backs, fussily collecting gloves and rugs and scarves. We couldn't push through these frail old folk to reach our children, and so we waited patiently. The boys would be all right, there were two of them; Robert would not be frightened while he had Niki to look after him.

But when the shuffling crowd had cleared, Robert had gone.

Niki said, 'He went to find Granny.'

As far as we knew, my mother was at home that afternoon. 'Did you *see* Granny?' we asked. It was conceivable that she might have decided to walk her dog to meet us. But Niki shook his head. In any case, she would not have taken Robert with her without telling us.

Austen's face was drained of colour. The bandstand was almost empty. We went to the box office. No, no one had seen a beautiful blond boy in a check Viyella blouse and navy knickers. Outside the bandstand, it was much colder. The beach was empty, a wide, shingly waste, and beyond the shingle, the shining blue mud stretched to the creaming edge of the sea. The promenade was almost empty, too; Uncle Jack's audience had not been tempted to linger in the bitter wind.

Niki began to cry. Then we saw Robert at the far end of the promenade – a tiny, vulnerable figure trotting between two larger people, two grown-ups, trustingly holding their hands as he was led away.

We ran. Austen reached them first. His angry bellow blew back on the wind. 'What are you doing with my son?'

His kidnappers turned: an old man, an old woman, looking both startled and relieved. The colour in their faces came from cold, not guilt. 'The little boy said his Mummy and Daddy had gone home and left him,' they explained. 'He said he wanted to find his Granny. He said she lived this way.'

Robert looked composed, indeed, complacent. There was no doubt that he had expressed himself clearly: he had spoken in structured sentences from the age of eighteen months. But his grandparents lived out of the town, about a mile away.

Perhaps he had run off to look for us, failed to find us, and then lost Niki, too. So being a sensible four-year-old, he took the hands of the first pair of kindly-looking grown-up servants to appear, and instructed them to take him home. But although we tried to find out what had happened so that we could take better care of him another time, he couldn't tell us. (He says, now, that he knew exactly what he was doing. He had asked his rescuers to take him to our car which was parked on the opposite side of the road, hardly any distance from the bandstand, and he meant to stand beside it and wait for us. He would have explained this to us at the time, he says, if we had not been so upset. He had been 'too busy dealing with our distress'.)

The child I wrote about in *Devil by the Sea* was older than my baby son, but I decided that the lack of communication between her and the adult world was much the same. I used a nine-year-old girl to give an extra turn of the screw to an adult thriller, turning Robert's innocent kidnappers into an inadequate outsider who murders one child out of fear and threatens others. The novel is set in Herne Bay as I knew it before and after the war, as a child and as an adult; sometimes, as I wrote it, I fancied I could smell seaweed and mud and wild, healthy, salty air.

Auntie Aggie (all good families have an Auntie Aggie) used to say that she liked my books because she always recognised the furniture. By which she meant, of course, not an actual chair or table, but surroundings, backgrounds, certain places. Certainly I used Herne Bay whenever I needed a run-down seaside town – why bother to invent when you have the props so near to hand? I had Herne Bay in mind when I wrote two children's books, *The Secret Passage* and *On the Run*, although when I needed chalk cliffs rather than wet and crumbly clay, I had to move to Birchington. And when I wanted a good aunt, in theatrical terms a 'reliable', there was always Peg, the eccentric comedian and nature lover whom I had once seen, in her pretty garden one mild spring night embrace a flowering apple tree.

Other useful 'furniture' was provided by the Thames valley where we lived while our family was growing up; commuter country, but with small towns that still had an identity, were not merely dormitories for

London. Local shops had been owned and run by the same families for years. A watchmaker with an amazing nose, covered with what looked like purple barnacles, seemed to have stepped straight out of a Dickens novel. A butcher who took his job so seriously that when we rang one Easter Saturday to say our turkey wasn't cooking as it should, he walked to our house in full butcher's fig of striped apron and straw hat, prodded the bird with his fork and said, 'Another half an hour.' Next door but one there was an empty tailor's shop where, within the memory of the two old ladies still living in the rooms above it, their father, the tailor, had once sat cross-legged in the window, and next to the tailor, a public house in which the snug was the nightly meeting place for all the Chertsey ironmongers. There was a well-stocked public library, good doctors and dentists and, behind our house, flat water meadows stretching to the river, a safe walk for children with blackberries in the hedgerows and country, not suburban, smells; may and dead nettle instead of laurel and privet.

And in Chertsey, there were still jobs for local people. Gravel pits circled the town, glimmering wastes of water surrounded by gaunt, naked machinery; a romantic industrial landscape that I found eerily beautiful. There had once been an abbey in Chertsey and it was said that the cellars beneath the old houses in London Street led into an underground hiding place used by the monks for clandestine meetings with nuns from the convent. There was certainly a way through from our house to the house next door; my sons discovered it one wet afternoon and ran triumphantly to tell me, filthy from wriggling on their bellies through a crumbling tunnel between one cellar and another.

I wrote my first children's book in Chertsey, calling it – unsurprisingly perhaps – *The Secret Passage*. I wrote it for a number of reasons, none of which I can remember clearly now. I know I was depressed by the books my sons were reading which seemed dull to me, chiefly because the characters were wooden, and uninvolved in any kind of reality I recognised. I think I wanted to give my children something that would encourage them to feel they could make a difference to what happened in the world, show them fictional children who were people like themselves, bright and gutsy and determined, able to think, to reason, to hold a moral view. And, what was perhaps more immediate and relevant, I had enjoyed writing about a nine-year-old in *Devil by the Sea* and been surprised how vividly my own childhood had come back to me.

On the other hand, to write *about* a child was, must be, different from writing a story that would engross a person of that age. I thought – in so far as I did think about it – that children's writers were likely to be specialists of one sort or another. But we were moving house, leaving Chertsey for Weybridge and I was busier than usual, clearing out the cellar which was silted up with close-packed rubbish like a long-abandoned archaeological site. Austen said, 'You like writing about children, why not write a book for them? It won't take you so long.'

It took a year, as had my adult novels, and no publisher wanted it when it was done. George Hardinge, who always stuck by me nobly as I changed direction (wilfully, it must have seemed to him sometimes, as I sought the voice I wanted to write in), did not publish books for children. My agent, Juliet O'Hea – the famous Queen of agents – said perhaps it was a bit *unusual* for a children's story. The mother died at the beginning, in a flood in Africa. Who was interested in Africa? The father had disappeared, deranged, it seemed, with grief. The children, sent to an apparently disagreeable aunt who ran a seaside boarding house, were poor and unhappy for a while. One of the characters was old and mad.

I said, 'At least it's not about rabbits wearing funny clothes.'

I put my failure behind me, moved house, settled the children in new schools, and wrote a novel about a family living in a near-derelict house on the edge of a gravel pit. Since I was clearly unable to write about real children *for* children, I determined to write about them for adults and the heroine of *Tortoise by Candlelight* was a fourteen-year-old girl who was a passionate defender of her disorganised family; a young, fierce, avenging angel. Both Emmie, in this novel, and the girl narrator of *A Little Love, A Little Learning*, are related, the kind of child I understood, and to some extent remembered being: turbulent and strong and loving. And the background is the same; Surrey suburbia at its leafy best, before motorways began to carve it up, at a time when there was still a good, local cottage hospital and quite young children could safely walk alone to school.

The Secret Passage was finally published by Livia Gollancz, who was starting up a children's list. That was in 1965 and it has not been out of print since then. I accepted an advance of £100, half on signature, half on publication, and thought myself lucky; an American publisher gave me an advance of $1,000. The adult novels were paying better by that time and I might not have written a second novel for children, if children had not sent me the kind of letters that surprised and delighted me. What had interested them in my story was what I had hoped would interest them. Not the plot, although they seemed to find it exciting enough, but the emotions, the feelings, of the characters. 'I didn't know,' they wrote, 'that other people felt like that.'

I thought – this is why *I* read novels! Of course children want a story just as I do, the gossipy power of *what happens next* to draw them into the world of the book, but what holds them, what their imaginations respond to, is its emotional landscape. To find someone in a book who shares your feelings, especially if they are shameful ones like jealousy or anger, is a comfort at any age. And for children, handicapped by ignorance and lack of control over their own lives, a book can show them the future, allow them to exercise, vicariously, the real power they will have one day.

I came to writing children's books by chance. It didn't occur to me that there should be any difference in approach, and although my first stories for children were conventional adventures, kidnappings, mysteries, and treasure found in caves on Scottish islands, I tried to make sure that the children in them should feel and think as children do. I wanted to write solid, grown-up novels for children; stories that treated them seriously, respecting their opinions and acknowledging the strength of their feelings. And, perhaps as a result, the plotting of the later books became less adventitious. *Carrie's War* and *Keeping Henry* are tales of love and loss that depend on a sequence of real events for their excitement.

For thirty years, from the great winter of 1963, when the Thames froze and there were ice floes on the sea at Herne Bay, I have written a children's book one year, an adult book the next. I find it a useful and satisfyingly frugal way of working; making use of all my life, all memory, wasting nothing. One leads to the other and, because of the difference between the child's and the adult's point of view, themes often overlap; an idea in a book for children will spark off an adult novel, and vice versa. *Squib* is a book for children which grew out of a case I had sat on in the magistrates' court: a request for a Place of Safety Order for a little boy who had been locked up in a rough shed at the end of the garden and tethered to the floor with a collar round his neck. Two smaller children, four and five, peering through the fence from the next-door garden, had known the boy was there for several days before they told their mother.

I wondered what they thought was going on; were they curious to see what would happen next, or had they been afraid to mention it in case it was a secret it was dangerous to tell? In *Squib* the eponymous child was rescued (inadvertently, and with the help of adults) by four different children, each acting out a separate fantasy about him, and when that book was finished I felt there should be more to say. What would happen to a child like Squib when he was fully grown, what sort of person would he become after such a desperate beginning? *Anna Apparent* is about a similar victim, a girl this time, a wartime evacuee abandoned and ill-treated on a Welsh hill farm, and is an attempt to understand what might happen to such a child in later life. It is a novel for adults about survival, and another character in it was based on a real-life survivor, Traute Kafka, who had married Derrick Sington, the journalist and broadcaster.

Derrick had been the first British Army intelligence officer to enter Belsen at the end of the war and he had met Traute there. She had been in one camp or another since the beginning of the war. She had survived Auschwitz and Theresienstadt and Hamburg; she said she had been lucky to have been young and a girl, lucky to have been strong enough to work, lucky to have had no children. She would not have survived long in Belsen but her luck held even there: the Allies liberated the camp ten days after her arrival.

Traute's history was terrible, and sometimes it amused her to tease the tender susceptibilities of her English friends with wryly comic stories that made her experience of war sound more like life in a jolly boarding-school than in the death camps of Europe. She had an unquenchable spirit that I tried to do justice to in *Anna Apparent*. If I failed, I did at least repeat her best story – and got lambasted for my truthful reporting. 'Tasteless', several critics said. But Traute laughed. And when I had finished that novel I remembered my own happier experiences as an evacuee in Wales, and thought of *Carrie's War*.

Sometimes I am not sure at the beginning on which side a book will fall. And sometimes, publishing a novel as a children's book is a matter of marketing. *The Peppermint Pig* is simply a story about family life at the turn of the century; I have had letters from adults who have read it without realising it was sold as a children's story. When I started *Carrie's War* I had not intended it for children; it was only slowly, as I wrote the first chapter, that I began to see the direction I was taking. And *The Real Plato Jones*, which is about a conflict of loyalties in wartime Greece and its repercussions fifty years later, could have been, written with a slightly different emphasis, a novel for adults.

Writing a novel *for* children had one effect on me: I began to stop writing *about* children for adults. There are children in *A Woman of My Age*, but they are off-stage, unseen. The central character is a woman in her thirties, trapped by domesticity, by two sons and a husband she is fond of but bored by. Travelling in Morocco, over the mountains and down to the desert, she rehearses her feelings, her political disagreements with her husband (they had quarrelled fiercely over Suez) and her own feeling of uselessness; she tells herself that life has little left to offer, 'now she has fulfilled her biological function'.

Elizabeth was not me, but her situation and feelings had once been mine. I was looking back at the person I had been about ten years before when I had left my first husband. In a way it was a 'key' book for me, as was *Carrie's War*. In both those novels I was mining my own remembered experiences more consciously and thoroughly than I had done before; using my own life to make a general statement that I hoped other people might understand and recognise.

Not that I thought of it like that. I was, as always, just trying to tell a good story that might interest and amuse someone else as well as me. But one of the pleasures of writing is putting your point of view across – using your characters as a ventriloquist does, or as shy or uncertain people do when they say, 'a friend of mine thinks', 'my husband says'. And to some extent I have identified with some of the women in some of my novels, even if it is hard to know how much of myself has actually gone into a particular female character. Once I have begun to write about, or through the eyes of, a woman of any age – projecting myself backwards in memory or forwards in speculation – she grows, develops mannerisms and attitudes that are not mine, becomes a person quite separate from me.

Laura, in *Walking Naked*, is living through a day that includes a Boat Race party, a game of real tennis at Hampton Court, a visit to her son in prison and to her father on his deathbed. Although I had lived through a similar day, a Boat Race party given by Sally and David Holloway, Austen's tennis game, visiting Niki in prison, and driving to Herne Bay to see my father (who had recovered before we got there) Laura is not me. It was simply that there was a comic awfulness about the unplanned but inevitable progression of that day's events that seemed to me too good to lie unused. And perhaps the father and the boy in prison bear a shadowy resemblance to my father and to Niki, but in the more complex characters there are only minor traces of real-life counterparts.

I was a magistrate from the middle 1960s until we moved to London in 1976. I was a political appointment, in the sense that the local Labour Party, asked to put forward a few names, had included mine. I was moderately astonished to be asked, even though it was fairly obvious that suitable leftish-winged candidates in our overwhelmingly Conservative Surrey suburb were likely to be rare. 'Must have been scraping the barrel,' I explained modestly when friends expressed their surprise at the unexpected turn my life had taken. I was torn between shame and embarrassment at being thought the sort of person who might belong even tangentially to the Establishment, and secret pride because I had been thought serious enough to be asked to join.

I bought a hat. I never wore it, but knowing that I owned one gave me the confidence of having a disguise to hand should it be needed. I went to a couple of training sessions, which taught me nothing much, sat in on several mornings' work in different courts, which I found more useful. I had expected to be bored; boredom, I thought, must necessarily accompany such a worthy occupation. Instead, I found the atmosphere and the proceedings riveting; a gripping serial drama.

The permanent cast of players included the bench, mostly middle-aged and conservative men and women, and a sprinkling of rather fierce trade unionists who were often surprisingly (surprising to me, that is) illiberal in their views. There was an engagingly handsome clerk, several elderly ushers with conventionally creaky shoes and a number of regularly attending policemen of all ages, the majority as honest as the day, and a few who lied, either out of habit or to get a conviction. These last were known to most of the bench and various delicate euphemisms were employed when we needed to disregard their evidence. There were guest appearances by probation officers, social workers, solicitors, and young barristers with their defendants, the reluctant stars without whom there would have been no play.

All criminal cases go first to a magistrates' court and 98 per cent are dealt with there: the untrained (and unpaid) members of the bench deciding the facts and the sentence, the clerk instructing them in the law. It is a demonstrably economical system and, given a well-balanced bench and a good clerk, a sensible one. Magistrates come in all shapes and sizes, clutching different sets of prejudices, stupidities, talents and virtues; given a spot of decent luck, a defendant has a reasonable chance of being fairly treated. In the nine years I was a magistrate, the worst injustices I saw were in the Crown Court, when I was sitting with a judge or a recorder, and a jury. Things went wrong, usually, because the defendant's barrister was incompetent, or because the judge was not sufficiently clear in his direction to the jury, or because the jury was stupid.

I see that I have given myself away in that last sentence. By things going 'wrong', I mean of course that the defendant did not get off when I thought he should have done. I like to think I was properly judicious, that I approved of the methods society uses to defend itself and, certainly, my heart did not bleed for professional criminals; thugs and thieves were thugs and thieves in my view, and not social victims. All the same, it was often the average defendant that I remembered most clearly from these legal theatricals, the defendant who had my secret empathy. Whatever the rights and wrongs of his case, by the time he gets into court he is already partly defenceless, worn down by waiting and worry, and the sight of a bench of sober citizens, or worse, a judge in a wig, will erode his defences still further. The routine of the court doesn't help him. He has to stand when he speaks to the bench. He has to give intimate details about himself and his life that he would prefer his closest friends not to know. Even if he is innocent he will begin to feel guilty. (I say 'he' and 'him' because there were always more men than women in the dock in my court; we had no regular prostitutes in our area and only a few female shoplifters.)

It was a case in the Crown Court in which the defendant was found guilty and given a suspended sentence, even though he had done nothing that any reasonable person could consider criminal – or even malicious or unkind – which made me decide that I had had enough. It was 1976, I was moving to London anyway, and I did not want to join the London Commission of the Peace. Niki had been imprisoned by a London court and I was quite murderously inclined towards the magistrates responsible. Although I did not really suppose that I would drop poison in their instant coffee if I was sent to serve in that court, it seemed best to avoid temptation. And, anyway, more seriously, it seemed to me that no one should be a lay magistrate for more than, say, ten years. Experience can stale. It can also lead to ignorant justices thinking that they know more than they do. Certainly, I had observed a regrettable bossiness in some of my colleagues who had been laying down the law too long, and thought it best to escape while I was still decently humble.

I wrote a book about being a magistrate and called it *Afternoon of a Good Woman*. Although a woman magistrate is the central character, her private life was more complex and murkier than mine. But alongside her story, which was pure invention, I made use of her to set down what being a magistrate was like for me, what had intrigued or repelled me. And, when the book was finished, I was surprised by how strongly I had felt. I had not realised until I wrote this novel how much I had disliked having all that frightening power. I had always enjoyed, not just the pageant of English life that passed before my fascinated eyes, but also the detective work of the court, listening to the evidence, making up my mind as to what had actually happened in this case or in that, and persuading other magistrates to see my point of view. What I had found uncomfortable – I think that *uncomfortable*, with its suggestion of mild, fastidious unease, is the right word for how I felt – was passing sentence, sending someone to prison, fining people more than they could afford, knowing they would be back in court in a month or two because they couldn't pay the fine. The margin of error that put me on the side of the judges and not of the judged sometimes seemed very narrow. It was against my nature, I told myself, to be one of the governing classes.

All the same, I expected to miss the work. Sitting in judgment on other people is a good deal easier than writing novels. It is also a task you don't need all your mind for all the time: there are long stretches while you are listening to the evidence when you can also be re-arranging and recycling a certain amount of what you are hearing for your private (in my case, literary) purposes. I had often found a day in court to be both relaxing and productive. But I didn't miss it for a moment when we moved to London. I missed our friends. I missed the piney air of Surrey. I missed the house that had room not only for our extended family of children but for our children's friends. I missed the garden. Nothing very interesting grew there because it was overhung with trees, but it was big enough for a roughish croquet lawn and we had had good games on summer evenings, bats flitting overhead, and children laughing.

One occasion I remember, we played another game. We had people to dinner. Among them was my sister-in-law's sister, Mary Hutchison, Simon Raven, who was staying with us, and Karl Miller, who was then editor of the *Listener*. It was Karl who wanted to play football and arranged the game. (There were ten of us; we were playing five-a-side.) Someone – Karl or Simon – asked Mary to be goalie.

Mary had just emerged from hospital after a mastectomy but although we tried to suggest that she should take another role, she laughed at us, and shook her head.

Austen and I came and went with drinks, watching the potatoes on the stove, keeping an anguished eye on Mary. She was still laughing. Karl seemed to be kicking the ball quite viciously and deliberately towards her, even to be aiming at her missing breast. He didn't know she had just come out of hospital, and since we hadn't told him to begin with (because we knew she didn't want it mentioned at this party) we were in greater difficulty as the game proceeded: the longer it went on, the more Karl would be mortified by his own behaviour in playing it so roughly.

Mary was not the only guest in trouble. Edward Ashcroft (Peggy Ashcroft's older brother who, until he retired, had been at the BBC with Austen) was purple in the face. Simon, too, was quite a pretty colour. Two heart attacks, I thought, as well as a frail young woman injured further. Well, the potatoes were cooked. I rang the dinner bell – an old school bell I had acquired from somewhere. No one took any notice. 'Stop this dreadful game,' I hissed at Simon who, performing some neat footwork with the ball, had come quite close to me. No luck. Perhaps he hadn't heard me. Austen, more effectively, began to collect all empty glasses; filled his lungs and yelled, 'Half time!'

No croquet in London in our pretty terrace house on the Regent Canal. We had only been able to afford it because there was a slump in the housing market in the mid-1970s. We paid £48,000 for the house, which had been built a hundred and thirty years before for up-and-coming city clerks, the kind of house that was increasingly being bought and 'gentrified' by people who could not afford more fashionable areas, Chelsea or Kensington. We peered through basement windows at fitted kitchens; dishwashers, steel sinks, blenders, stripped pine furniture. Some houses were abandoned, doors and windows boarded up, but in others that seemed just as derelict people were still living; tending woody geraniums in leaky window-boxes, putting out plastic bags of garbage on the crumbling steps. It was an area where comparatively rich and almost-poor lived side by side, where old London met new London; in Chapel Street market, plump women in saris and dark, handsome men in turbans mingled with the stable population of indigenous cockneys, Poles and Italians, and with the professional in-comers, the lawyers, literary agents, television presenters, journalists and politicians.

It was, and is, a lively place, so densely peopled that surges of pedestrians sometimes stopped the traffic in the main street. If in some moods I was cast down by the pot-holed pavements and the dirty streets, the yellow foam that streaked the brown canal, the dead cats and the rotten fruit that bobbed against the closed gates of the lock, in others I was enchanted by the friendliness of strangers in this part of the inner city, by the exotic variety of the faces in the streets and shops. And by the beauty of the urban landscape. From our bedroom on the fifth floor we could see a great sweep of sky, the graceful skeletons of yellow cranes marking the site of a new office block near the tube station, the delicate spires of small City churches, the gold figure of Justice on the Old Bailey, the grey helmet of the dome of St Paul's, the ferocious Barbican tower blocks, rearing up like jagged-toothed dinosaurs, the faint strokes, pencil thin, of more cranes, far away at the docks, beyond the gin factory. That was at dawn, in daylight; at night, even the ugliest tower blocks turned into fairy palaces.

Both moods, dolorous and elevated, were useful in setting scenes for *Familiar Passions* and *The Ice House*, the background of one moving from Surrey to Islington to Shropshire, and the other coming to a climax in Egypt, on the Nile, but mostly taking place in London. Bridie Starr, the heroine of *Familiar Passions*, discarded by her much older and quite loathsome husband (who like all horrid characters, was an especial joy to invent and write about), retreats to a flat in Islington, which has temporarily been vacated by one of her psychiatrist father's madder patients. She finds herself wretchedly displaced, suffering all the pangs of bewilderment and loss that I felt myself when we first moved from Surrey, and begins to recover on a nostalgic journey of self-discovery that takes her from Shropshire to South Wales.

Economical as always, I also used Islington for a children's book, *The Robbers*, and for *Family Money*, where the setting was also the subject of the novel. Spread over three generations, the natural history of any family is a good way to focus on social and economic change. When I was young, owning your house was not a national obsession. Most poor people rented; it was not until after the First World War that the very slightly better off might buy, as my parents did, on the never-never. By the 1950s, houses cost only a little more than they would have done before the war, and I can remember my first husband (who inherited that £30,000), speaking with pity about a cousin whose parents had recently died, saying that he wouldn't 'come into' anything because his uncle and aunt had nothing to leave except the house they were living in. That house, in a wooded suburb, with a tennis court and five bedrooms, would probably have sold for between four and five thousand pounds, a price that was to be much the same twenty years later.

By the late 1980s, however, things had changed and the greedy and fascinated gaze of the English home-owning classes became riveted on the apparently unstoppable rise in house prices. Our house was 'worth' half a million by 1990. There was an innocent pleasure in contemplating the huge profit made by simply sitting still and letting time pass but it made no practical difference to most of us: people need to live somewhere and if they are living in a house and want to sell it, they have to buy another. (Renting, so common in Europe among the middle classes, is considered, in England, only an option for the poor.) The real social change, both for individuals and the economy in general, was when the parents of middle-aged house-owners died, turning families who had no other money into capitalists for the first time. In the future, a large number of people were going to be concerned, as only a few had once been, in the old excitements of wills and inheritance, the arguments over *Family Money*.

I was pleased with this novel. It gathered together various ideas, themes, that I enjoy writing about: the depth and complexity of internecine family quarrels; the effects of a shattering event on behaviour and the way we see other people; the use of a landscape – in this case a townscape – as part of the narrative. And, because I am reluctantly drawn to the notion that darkness and chaos threaten us all, lying in wait at the bottom of the garden, lurking outside the safe, lighted room, I placed my heroine, Fanny, in a frightening situation, one that frightened me, certainly, and gave her the courage (the kind of courage I would like to think I might have myself in similar circumstances) to find a way out of it.

Writing is not a lonely occupation as is sometimes said – *lonely* has a plaintive sound to it, a suggestion of complaint – but it is a solitary one. In London, especially after Niki died, I was sometimes bored by my own company. I had been reviewing new novels every few weeks for David Holloway, the magisterial literary editor of the *Daily Telegraph*, and instead of waiting for a parcel to arrive, began to pick up the books myself. David was a good man to work for, stern and indulgent in the right proportions, and I looked forward to my monthly trips to Fleet Street, feeling I was at last brushing shoulders with the romantic world I had aspired to since Uncle Stanley gave me my first typewriter.

And I was glad to serve on various writers' committees, PEN, the Society of Authors, the Royal Society of Literature. All excellent institutions and even if I was never really sorry when my time came to an end, that was only because I felt I was not a naturally useful committee person, being given to wandering thoughts and general inattentiveness. But I was pleased to have played a modest part in the campaign for Public Lending Right, and flattered to be asked to follow in the footsteps of Joyce Grenfell as president of the Society of Women Writers and Journalists: a friendly and very practical society, set up in the 1890s by a gentlemanly editor who was concerned that women journalists had no club of their own.

Each of these organisations has its own flavour; if, occasionally, one of them is riven by passionate politicking, it is only fascinating to those involved and incomprehensible, except as a paradigm, to the rest of the world. The same is true of professional conferences, although I suspect that conferences of writers are intrinsically more comic than conferences of doctors or dentists or sculptors or engineers who presumably have practical things to discuss. Writers, like politicians, can only pass resolutions.

Although conferences organised by International PEN have their valuably serious side, notably as an effective pressure group on governments that imprison their dissident writers, there is also an agreeable amount of junketing; parties and expeditions arranged by the host country, which the participants enjoy or not depending on their temperaments. I think of an occasion in the Ivory Coast when the bus that had taken a group of staid and mainly middle-aged poets and novelists to a village up country, took a short cut home and sank to a muddy standstill in the jungle. Those who had been properly appreciative of the village hospitality (palm wine and French champagne) leapt from their seats and pushed; two usefully powerful Russians, who had drunk particularly deep, melodiously singing the Volga Boatmen song. Others remained on the bus and fumed. The International Secretary, a formidable personage who had once been an opera singer, sat squarely in his seat and spoke with wonderfully measured disgust. 'I advised against Africa.'

Conference comedies and scandals are usually more comic or riveting to the participants at the time than they appear in retrospect. The chemistry produced when a disparate group of grown-ups are gathered together seems to reduce them from independent, articulate adults to an artificial childhood. Foolish jokes are treasured. Most people drink more than they should. Couplings, intrigues and feuds that would take months to develop and work through outside, in the real world, are speeded up by some unseen and relentless finger on the fast-forward button. There are weird conflicts of culture. An elderly friend of mine was propositioned by a very young Macedonian poet. She was a tough and merry widow in her mid-seventies with an enviable string of much younger lovers, but even she thought this particular age gap too great. The poet was desperate – not with love or lust – but with shame: his dignity as a man was at stake. By refusing him, he reproached her, she had injured his honour and his health. He had had to spend the night hiding in the hotel lounge in case his room-mate should find out, and he had caught a nasty chesty cold.

When writers are gathered together, they discuss money: advances, royalties, the advantages of being registered for VAT. It seems to me (and I can only speak for myself) that it is rare for writers to talk about their work with each other. A kind of shyness prevents me from asking even good friends about their writing. And all I can ever say to them about my current novel is how many thousand words I have got down on paper. Perhaps biographers are different. Because their subject has an independent existence they can talk around it without dissipating its energy. A half-completed novel is in a much more delicate condition; to give birth prematurely is to lose it. I fear so, anyway.

On the other hand, I am happy to talk about my finished work to strangers; to librarians or teachers about the children's books, about the adult novels at literary festivals. 'Showing off', I call these occasions, modestly disclaiming any special skill, only the family liking for drama that seems to run in a straight line from my grandfather, the coach painter (who embarrassed his children by leaping from his seat at the end of a good film and waving his arms and shouting *Bravo* as if he were in a live theatre), through my Aunt Peg, through Perdita, who used to be Steve Berkoff's company manager, to my grandson, Sam, and my granddaughter, Ottilie. It is something to do with the almost tangible excitement of feeling a response from an audience – especially gratifying if you are reading from your own work. And an even greater compliment than laughter is to see someone wipe away a tear.

Perhaps because of this theatrical streak, I have always been simply and straightforwardly pleased when my books have been adapted for film or television. I like to see what someone else has made of my characters, even if they are portrayed so successfully on screen that I forget how they first appeared in my imagination. The male narrator of *Circles of Deceit* will always be Edward Fox to me because Edward played him so convincingly that the somewhat clumsier and considerably less patrician person that I had originally imagined, faded from my mind. And that fierce and splendid actress, Rosalie Crutchley, cast as Hepzibah in *Carrie's War*, vanquished my plumper Hepzibah, who had a paler, pink and white complexion, and a gentle, sing-song voice.

I was only once embarrassed by an adaptation and that was long ago. *The Solitary Child* came out in 1956 – in what I still think of as Suez year. We were not poor, exactly, but we had more bills than we could pay. Just before Christmas I had a call from Curtis Brown to say that they had had an offer of £500 for the film rights and I was overjoyed. We could buy presents for our children, we could pay the butcher, we could even pay the mortgage! I was astounded when the voice on the telephone said we should hold out for a better offer. If the film company had to pay me more, the argument ran, they would put more into the production to make sure they got their money back. I saw our rich Christmas vanishing. No, I said, £500 will suit me very nicely. And I want it now.

We bought the children splendid presents, we paid the butcher *and* the grocer. We paid the mortgage and we had a bit of money over. But they made a B-feature film of my novel and no doubt it served me right.

The night before the press showing we were to dine with George Hardinge, at the French Club in St James's. I left the children with the babysitter and drove, through heavy fog, to London. I collected Austen from Bush House and we went to George's flat. I had a gin and tonic – a strong one, but I sipped it cautiously. We went to the French Club and, before I had touched a drop of wine, I fainted. When I came round, I couldn't stand. I must have seemed quite drunk – tippling the sauce all afternoon, most likely. George, who is a deeply chivalrous man, did not mention this possibility. And, although it naturally leapt to my husband's chagrined mind, the truth was that I had suddenly and inexplicably developed an allergy to alcohol. I didn't – couldn't – touch the stuff for several years.

The next morning I seemed to have slept it off. I went to the press showing of *The Solitary Child*. Austen (wisely, it turned out) had said he could not come and I had decided to take my Auntie Aggie with me as a treat. It was hard on her. I thought the film was dreadful. Margaret Lockwood's daughter featured in it, and a handsome, slightly stolid actor, called Paul Carpenter. Sitting in the circle, next to Auntie who kept saying soothing things like, 'Don't worry, sweetheart, I expect it will get better', I recalled the terrible occasion when my African play about elephant hunters had been performed at my primary school. Humiliation, past and present, overtook me. I fainted – no, *pretended* to faint – and was carted out by members of the press who were doubtless equally glad to escape from the inept drama on the screen. I kept my eyes squeezed shut until Auntie Aggie's piteously imploring cries aroused my better nature. I came back to life for her sake.

I was glad she was the only witness to my shame. I was convinced that if any publisher saw this dreadful film my writing career would be over. No one would take me seriously again. For days I scanned the newspapers for cruel and mocking notices. Luckily no one saw fit even to mention *The Solitary Child* and my panic – which was a physically painful, heart-thumping, lump-in-throat terror – slowly died away. Years later, by chance, I saw the film on television. My sons had turned it on one evening and made me watch it with them. It was a low-budget, B-feature movie, unremarkable but competent. Nothing to be ashamed of, after all.

When he was a young man, my American publisher, Cass Canfield, walked across China. He had been to Harvard and was to go to Oxford; in between he took a steamer to Rangoon and walked from there, guided by the only map he could find, which was the one Marco Polo had used. He had another young American with him but at some point they separated and Cass walked on alone, towards Canton. This was the early 1920s, the time of the warlords. In one village he was told to hire soldiers to protect him on the next leg of the journey. They walked all day and stopped to camp for the night at the end of a ravine. When Cass woke in the morning the soldiers had vanished, taking with them the little food he was carrying.

Better to go on than turn back, he decided. He set off at a smart pace into the ravine. A stone dropped in front of him, spitting dust, and he looked up to see bayonets glinting above him. He was unarmed. He was young. Fate had never harmed him. He lifted a hand in greeting and shouted 'Hi.' And the bandits came down, made him coffee, escorted him to the next village and warned him not to travel alone again.

Cass was old by the time that I knew him but he was easy to imagine young. He was a rich, successful and charmingly old-fashioned publisher; he published the books that he liked and there was a staircase, not a lift, in his office building. He always sent yellow roses to my hotel when I arrived in New York and his chauffeur, Robert, always collected me from the airport. One evening, after dinner, Cass said I should see Chinatown. His wife protested it wasn't safe to walk there at night. He said, 'But of course Robert will be with us.' And so, as we walked through the brilliant city, the Cadillac whispered a yard behind us.

Cass's publishing house, Harper and Row, bought the general list of J.B. Lippincott, who published my children's books. Harper moved from the building with the staircase to a skyscraper with lifts. Accountants took over. Cass was too grand to be affected; he had an enormous office and kept a few of his favoured authors. I was among them, as was Isaac Bashevis Singer, and we were passed down to the lower levels of the firm like tablets from on high. This was good for my self-esteem but it may have created resentment. When Cass finally retired, to general sorrow, the woman who took over his list turned down my next novel, *Familiar Passions*, saying quite rightly that it was not *The Thorn Birds*. My agent protested and, the next time I was in New York, sent me to see a man called Ed Burlinghame who had become the new Harper overlord. He said that if I were to come to Harper and Row with my next children's book, they would continue to publish my adult novels. I stalked out with my nose in the air. (At least, that is how I choose to recollect the occasion.)

Although the American editions of my children's books had always been published by Lippincott, when Lippincott was bought by Harper and Row my editor (and close friend) Dorothy Briley, left to go to Lothrop, Lee and Shephard which was part of William Morrow. I followed her then, as I followed her later, from Lothrop to Clarion Books, owned by Houghton Mifflin. Not much of a saga as publishing histories go, nowadays, but it demonstrates a trend which would have been rare twenty years earlier. Once upon a happy time, editors stayed with the same publisher throughout their working life and writers stayed with their editors. Now, as publishers merge, or are bought up by finance houses or sugar manufacturers, editors flit from one house to another and their writers trail after them, lost sheep after a wandering shepherd.

In England I clung to George Hardinge's elegant coat tails as he moved from Collins, to Longman's, and then to Macmillan's. He published my adult novels from 1954 to 1987 and was the most professional of publishers as well as the best of friends. George was a founder member of the Booker Prize for Fiction, the annual razzmatazz that has become as much a part of routine English life as chocolate eggs on Easter Sunday. For a short-listed novelist who doesn't win, it may be painful: you need a hardy nature to sit through a boozy dinner, pretending you don't mind if you win or lose, and for a judge who sees her brilliant choice rejected for an inferior offering it is even worse, a desperate, teeth-grinding frustration. (I have been in both positions, so I know.) But it has meant that for one night in the year, novels are seen to be taken at least halfway seriously, and one fortunate scribbler is richer for it.

The best recipe for a healthy old age is not eating muesli, or drinking carrot juice, or jogging, but being born to healthy, long-lived parents. Publishers and agents may not be an exact analogy, but it will serve. George Hardinge was my publisher for thirty years; Juliet O'Hea, my agent for almost as long. At Gollancz, Joanna Goldsworthy published my children's books and one adult novel. When Juliet retired she passed me on to Michael Shaw, a stout defender of his authors, and before Joanna left Gollancz for Transworld, she handed me over to Lynn Knight at Virago, who now publish my novels. Since all the children's books are still in print in Puffin paperback, and my American editions lovingly cared for by Dorothy Briley in America, I am a fortunate writer. But like a strong old person born with sturdy genes, I owe a lot to the initial luck of having people to publish and support me who liked my work and gave me courage to go on.

Envoi

Cass Canfield once said, 'Nina, dear, why do you *gallop* at the end of novels. It's as if, the end in sight, you take the bit between your teeth, lay your ears back, and *hurl* yourself into the straight.'

Well, maybe. Perhaps I gallop because I feel I have said all that I have to say. There is no proper finish for a novel, other than death or marriage; an autobiography does not even have that choice. Unless you can arrange to gasp the last sentence on your deathbed, you are in an uncertain position. I could die tomorrow, slip on the ice, fall under a Number 19 bus. But at the moment there is no right, true end. I am alive and healthy and making cautious plans. And in those plans the pleasures and rewards of doing something as well as I can do it, still figure boldly.

Daring to look at my work as a whole, and taking it seriously as I would take the work of another writer unknown to me, I seem to discern a social and political sub-text whispering on through all the novels, a sub-text that a sociologist might call the rise and fall of the welfare state. The doctor-stepfather in *A Little Love, A Little Learning*, and the submerged but battling heroine of *A Woman of My Age*, who deceives her husband, not because she has a lover, but because she is attending a Labour Party meeting, both assume that the value of public service is accepted by all good people without question. The parents in *The Birds on the Trees*, who have a son expelled from school for taking drugs in the sixties, are finding out (as we found out, indeed) that the cradle-to-grave safety net has enormous holes in it. The travel agent in *George beneath a Paper Moon* makes a fortune, cashing in at the beginning of the package deal boom, and *Family Money* is set at the end of the disastrous Thatcher decade when the idea of working for the public good was disparaged, and buying and selling your family home was a smart way to make money.

I try to make sense of the times I have lived through by writing stories. All my novels, including the children's books, if read in sequence would provide (for me, at any rate) a kind of coded autobiography. It is not that I have always written about myself, although of course all writers write about themselves to some extent, just that everywhere, slipped in – often without my noticing it until after the book was published – there is something discussed or commented on that was of passionate interest to me at the time. And sometimes it seems that I only understand what I really think and feel when I see what I have written. I didn't know how much I hated sitting in judgment on other people until I had finished *Afternoon of a Good Woman*. And in a later novel, playing a minor role, there is a schizophrenic boy whom I had never intended to include in the story.

A writer's work may be a coded autobiography, but only a very close friend could decipher it. Niki was already dead when I wrote *Circles of Deceit*, but once my gentle schizophrenic had slipped into the story (as the son of the painter-narrator) I decided he could stay. I thought his death would make a moving and a fitting climax. But when it came to it, I found I couldn't bear to let him die in a book, and so I managed to save him until the last page was written, even though I hinted that he might not last long.

And, I have to admit it, keeping him alive made a more effective ending . . .

All writers are liars. They twist events to suit themselves. They make use of their own tragedies to make a better story. They batten on their relations. They are terrible people. They 'put people in books' – although by the time the book is under way they are honestly convinced that the character they are writing about has sprung entirely from their imagination. Writers are not to be trusted. Except in one thing. Most of us try to do our best for the sake of the story and try to be true, not to ourselves because that would be a hopeless task, but to the tale we are telling.

Also by Nina Bawden

A NICE CHANGE

'Pure bliss' – *Evening Standard*

'Compelling drama. Often comic, always intriguing, it's a perfect study of tangled emotions among a group of disparate people thrown together at random. I loved it' – *Good Housekeeping*

'A gently entertaining tale of summer love and Brits abroad . . . An accomplished storyteller with considerable emotional insight. Vintage stuff' – *Harpers and Queen*

'An elegantly written, happy, sun-filled novel set in her beloved Greece' – **P.D. James,** *Sunday Times*

Amy thought The Hotel Parthenon in Greece would be a nice change for her husband, Labour MP Tom Jones. He is convinced it's a bad idea as soon as they arrive and he spots Portia, his ex-mistress, in the minibus to the hotel. Also on board are Philip, an American publisher, the young Dr Prudence Honey, Beryl and 'Daddy' Boot from London and the two enigmatic, elderly twins Jane and Tish. The scene is set for a wonderful comedy told with the ironic humour and compassion Nina Bawden's readers have come to know her by. This is the author's latest novel.

FAMILIAR PASSIONS

'Nina Bawden deals out her ironic shocks with
scrupulous timing; the reader is thoroughly entranced
and entertained' – *Times Literary Supplement*

After an expensive dinner on their thirteenth wedding
anniversary, James calmly announces that he wishes to
leave Bridie. A cherished adopted child, she stepped into
marriage – and a pet name – at the age of nineteen.
Now, redundant and with her happiness turned into a
charade, she is uncertain of her identity. Here, with her
characteristic wit and acuity, Nina Bawden peers into
the familiar passions of family life, remembered insults,
ancient scars and old deceptions.

FAMILY MONEY

'Nina Bawden's readers should be numbered like the sands of the sea . . . This is a wonderfully satisfying novel, wise, tolerant, witty' – *Guardian*

Nina Bawden's successor to the Booker shortlisted *Circles of Deceit*, is a tale about families, old age and money. Fanny Pye's London house is now worth half a million pounds, so when she is hospitalised after a violent street brawl her children suggest that she move and thereby release some 'family money'. Fanny is more concerned that she cannot remember the terrible incident in which a man died. As her amnesia clears, Fanny realises that she is in danger . . . Here, the tempo of a thriller is brilliantly linked with a wry examination of the manners and morals of an acquisitive society.

GEORGE BENEATH A PAPER MOON

'I like it as much as any novel I've read this year. The comedy lies, as in the best and subtlest of comedies, in the exquisite patterning, the way in which events bounce and reverberate' – *New Statesman*

George is an unusually successful travel agent, providing other people with the adventures he dare not risk. Though content to wrap himself in fantasies, he is haunted by the belief that he fathered the daughter of his best friends. A holiday in Turkey snaps his private world when George finds himself in the midst of intrigue and murder and is forced to acknowledge that life is not the fairy-tale he'd imagined. In this superbly constructed and mercilessly observed novel – part comedy, part thriller – Nina Bawden exposes the fictions we impose on our lives.

THE ICE HOUSE

'Nina Bawden's great talent is to be able to take you along a perfectly ordinary street, rip the façade away and show the strange and passionate events that go on behind closed doors' – *Daily Telegraph*

At fifteen, Daisy, confident and cherished, is appalled to hear that Ruth's father locked her in the old garden ice house as a childhood punishment. The revelation of that primitive cruelty cements a friendship to last for many years. Friendship, love, marriage and, above all, the scorching effects of adultery, come under the microscope in this dextrous novel. Journeying from a terrifying suburban household to its unexpected conclusion in the Egyptian Pharaohs' tombs, *The Ice House* is startling, tragic and humorous by turns.

ANNA APPARENT

'A born story-teller' – *Independent*

Who is Anna? Is she Annie-May Gates, the war-time
evacuee who encounters neglect and unwitting abuse on
a Welsh farm? Giles's shy child-bride? Conscientious
mother and housewife? Or Daniel's undemanding but
sophisticated mistress? It takes catastrophe and a
gripping twist of plot for Anna to emerge as an
individual. Nina Bawden delves skilfully into character
and offers the richly textured story of a woman's life and
strategems, and of the flawed, kindly people who
surround her.

TORTOISE BY CANDLELIGHT

'An exceptional picture of disorganised family life . . .
Imaginative, tender, with a welcome undercurrent of
toughness' – *Observer*

With the ferocity of a mother tiger defending her cubs,
fourteen-year-old Emmie Bean watches over her
household: her amiable drunken father, her evangelical
grandmother, her wayward sister Alice and, most
precious of all, eight-year-old Oliver, who has the
countenance of an angel and the ethical sense of a cobra.
But with the arrival of new neighbours, the outside world
intrudes into family life and Emmie fights to stave off
the changes – and the revelations – that growing up
necessarily brings. Powerful, heart-rending, but never
sentimental, *Tortoise by Candlelight* is a captivating
excursion into the landscape of youth.

WALKING NAKED

'Her heroine stands before us . . . a looking glass through which to see ourselves' – *Cosmopolitan*

Laura is happily married, a mother and a successful novelist. Although she is prey to night terrors, she is adept at smoothing the disorder of reality into controlled prose. *Walking Naked* telescopes the whole of Laura's life into a day in which the past and present converge. Beginning with a game of tennis played for duty rather than amusement it progresses, via an afternoon party of old friends and jaded emotions, to a bewildering visit to Laura's son, imprisoned on a drugs' charge. At its close, the possibility of a death within the family hauls unresolved conflicts centre stage and Laura strips herself of the posturing and self-deceit with which she has cloaked her vulnerability.

A WOMAN OF MY AGE

'Rarely have the workings of a woman's mind been revealed with such clarity' – *Daily Telegraph*

Elizabeth and Richard, eighteen years married, have come to Morocco on holiday. As the adventures and disasters of their travels unfold, so too does Elizabeth's account of the desert her life has become. Her grievances and frustrations are credible and sympathetically told, yet, simultaneously and subversively, Nina Bawden demonstrates the inevitable ambivalences and deceptions within marriage. As the story moves towards a shocking catastrophe and an extremely surprising coda, Nina Bawden deploys her themes – marriage, families, expectations and betrayals – with poise, wit and charm, and proves once again that there is no more subtle chronicler of the human heart.

Now you can order superb titles directly from Virago

☐	Anna Apparent	Nina Bawden	£6.99
☐	The Birds on the Trees	Nina Bawden	£4.99
☐	Familiar Passions	Nina Bawden	£5.99
☐	Family Money	Nina Bawden	£5.99
☐	George Beneath a Paper Moon	Nina Bawden	£6.99
☐	Grain of Truth	Nina Bawden	£5.99
☐	The Ice House	Nina Bawden	£5.99
☐	A Little Love, A Little Learning	Nina Bawden	£5.99
☐	Tortoise by Candlelight	Nina Bawden	£5.99
☐	Walking Naked	Nina Bawden	£5.99
☐	A Woman of My Age	Nina Bawden	£5.99

Please allow for postage and packing: **Free UK delivery**.
Europe; add 25% of retail price; Rest of World; 45% of retail price.

To order any of the above or any other Virago titles, please call our credit card orderline or fill in this coupon and send/fax it to:

Virago, 250 Western Avenue, London, W3 6XZ, UK.
Fax 0181 324 5678   Telephone 0181 324 5516

☐ I enclose a UK bank cheque made payable to Virago for £..............

☐ Please charge £.............. to my Access, Visa, Delta, Switch Card No.

☐☐☐☐☐☐☐☐☐☐☐☐☐☐☐☐☐☐☐

Expiry Date ☐☐☐☐   Switch Issue No.   ☐☐

NAME (Block letters please) ....

ADDRESS ....

....

....

Postcode ....Telephone ....

Signature ....

Please allow 28 days for delivery within the UK. Offer subject to price and availability.

Please do not send any further mailings from companies carefully selected by Virago ☐